THE
EXOTICS

THE
EXOTICS

Being a Collection of
Unique Personalities and
Remarkable Characters

by MORRIS BISHOP

American Heritage Press · New York

Contents

The admirable James Crichton

1 The Admirable Crichton

"I have decided to be admirable, in all, for all," said Cyrano de Bergerac in Rostand's play. He spoke for the Renaissance man, whose ambitions knew no bounds; for Pico della Mirandola, that comely cavalier who proposed to defend nine hundred theses on mathematics, theology, and scholastic subjects; for Leon Battista Alberti, architect, artist, musician, author, who could tame the wildest horse and the wildest woman, and jump over a man's head from an immobile stance; for Leonardo himself. Cyrano spoke also for the Admirable Crichton, ill-fated Mirror of Perfection.

James Crichton was born on August 19, 1560, in Dumfriesshire. He was the son of Robert Crichton, who became Lord Advocate of Scotland. A prodigy, the boy entered St. Andrews University at ten, and received his B.A. at twelve (or thirteen), his M.A. two years later. He must have spent the next few years in raging study and self-cultivation, for we soon find him in possession of twelve languages (Pico had claimed twenty-two), of the profundities of scholarship, and of uncommon athletic skill and courtly grace. He was aided in his intellectual pursuits by an extraordinary memory. He could repeat verbatim anything he had ever read, could even, on demand, recite verse backward. He is described as tall, handsome, blond, blue-eyed, trimly bearded. At some time in his troubled teens he was converted to Romanism and was ordered out of Scotland by his angry father. He went to France and served in the army.

Now fact takes on the adornments of fancy. Many of the adornments are supplied by his fantastic biographer, Sir Thomas Urquhart, who made the ever memorable translation of Rabelais, who contrived a universal language in which every word could be read backward or forward, and who, it is said, died of a fit of laughter on learning that King Charles II of England was restored to his throne.

According to Sir Thomas, Crichton posted notices throughout Paris, challenging all comers to dispute with him on a certain day on any science, liberal art, or discipline, whether metaphysical, arithmetical, geometrical, astronomical, musical, optical, cosmographical, trigonometrical, or statistical, whether in Hebrew, Syriac, Arabic, Greek, Latin, Spanish, French, Italian, English, Dutch, Flemish, or Slavonian, in verse or prose at the disputant's choice. All the rarest minds of Paris set themselves to prepare pitfalls for the overweening challenger. "All this while, the Admirable Scot (for so from henceforth he was called) minding more his hawking, hunting, tilting, vaulting, riding of well-managed horses, tossing of the pike ... flourishing of colors, dancing, fencing, swimming, jumping, throwing of the bar, playing at the tennis, balloon, or long-catch ... playing at the chess, billiards, trou madame, and other suchlike chamber-sports, singing, playing on the lute and other musical instruments, masking, balling, reveling, and ... being more addicted to and plying closer the courting of handsome ladies and a jovial cup in the company of bacchanalian blades than. . . ." (Sir Thomas extricates himself from his sentence a page further on.)

On the appointed day the rector of the university gave the word to his learned champions to "fall on." They argued of everything knowable, *de omni scibili*; but the incomparable Crichton confounded them all "and publicly evidenced such an universality of knowledge and accurate promptness in re- solving of doubts, distinguishing of obscurities, expressing the members of a distinction in adequate terms of art . . . [that] with all excogitable variety of learning . . . [he] entertained . . . the nimble-witted Parisians from nine o'clock in the morning till six at night." The rector then favored him with a panegyric speech of half an hour's continuance and presented him with a diamond ring and a purse of gold. "There was so great a plaudite in the school, such a humming and clapping of hands, that all the concavities of the colleges thereabout did resound with the echo of the noise thereof." The next day, to refresh his brains, Crichton went to the Louvre and gave an exhibition of horse- manship, picking off the ring with his lance fifteen times in succession.

Unfortunately, no one so far has discovered any corrobo- ration of this great joust of erudition, wit, and dexterity. No doubt the silence of the Parisian pundits is due to shame.

There is, however, no question that Crichton appeared in Genoa, destitute, in July, 1579. He addressed the senate in a Latin speech, which was published. But as the businesslike Genoese proffered no gold-filled purses, he pushed on to Venice. The records of the ruling Council of Ten report, on August 19, 1580, the arrival of James Crichton, Scottish noble of rare and singular attainments. He gave a public extempore Latin oration and "filled the minds of all with astonishment and stupor." The Council gratified him with one hundred gold crowns, a hand- some lecture fee in any era. Various testimonies refer to him as a monster of learning, a miracle of perfection whose only peer was Alexander the Great; he outdid the learned in learning, the gallants in notable seductions. A printed handbill, which per- haps he prompted, calls him a prodigy of prodigies, who has Aristotle and the commentators at his fingers' ends and Thomas

Aquinas and Duns Scotus by heart. The handbill says that he has disputed with the Greeks on the procession of the Holy Ghost. And now he has retired to a villa to prepare two thousand propositions, which he will defend in the church of St. John and St. Paul in two months' time.

Crichton's charm subjugated Aldus Manutius the second, the famous Venetian scholar-printer who had begun publishing at nine. Aldus dedicated to Crichton his *Paradoxa Ciceronis*, with a high-flown liminary epistle reporting that Crichton had revealed the errors of Aristotle in a three-day orgy of scholarship, answering his opponents either by logical and ordinary methods or by the secret devices of astronomy or in mathematical, poetic, and other forms, at their choice. People thronged to his exhibitions as they did to hear Plato when he debarked from Sicily and emptied the stands at the Olympic Games.

(The proposal of theses and their defense as a sporting event were a feature of medieval scholasticism; the announcement that Abelard would take on all comers could fill a cathedral. The Renaissance exaggerated, as was its wont. Crichton's contemporary Giacomo Mazzoni proposed to defend 5,197 propositions on Aristotle and Plato. Luther's 95 theses tacked on the door of Wittenberg church were a mere trifle. The scholarly challenge, which has dwindled to angry "Letters to the Editor," would perhaps be worth reviving.)

After an unfruitful stay in Padua, where he delivered an extempore oration in praise of ignorance, as if "to reconcile his audience to their comparative inferiority," Crichton moved to Mantua. The city and territory were ruled by the old, bigoted Duke Guglielmo Gonzaga; his son and heir, Vincenzo, just twenty, was a bully, bravo, and lecher in the Renaissance tradition, and the terror of the city.

According to Sir Thomas Urquhart, my unreliable darling, Crichton challenged and defeated a swaggering furioso, spitting him neatly so as to describe a perfect isosceles triangle on his breast. Further, says Sir Thomas, Crichton produced a play of his own for the carnival. He took all fifteen parts in a performance that lasted five hours. One of the maids of honor ruptured a vein laughing. And he won the favors of a lady besought by Prince Vincenzo. The love scene is majestic, though verging on the indelicate: ". . . the visuriency of either, by ushering the tacturiency of both, made the attrectation of both consequent to the inspection of either: here it was that Passion was active, and Action passive; they both being overcome by other, and each the conqueror. To speak of her *hirquitalliency* at the *elevation* of the *pole* of his Microcosm, or of his luxuriousness to erect a *gnomon* on her *horizontal* dial, will perhaps be held by some to be expressions full of obsceneness, and offensive to the purity of chaste ears."

According to Sir Thomas, Crichton was interrupted in his dalliance by the jealous Prince Vincenzo. It is possible; but we had best abandon Sir Thomas for the inquest on the subsequent events. The prince testified that at one in the morning he was taking the fresh air with a companion. Mistaking a hooded passerby for a friend, he jostled him in jest and brought him to the ground. The figure, Crichton, rose and stabbed the prince's companion in the back. The prince engaged Crichton and delivered a happy thrust. Crichton, recognizing royalty, begged his pardon and died, as did the prince's companion.

Duke Guglielmo was furious at the loss of a man "famous throughout the world." The prince was officially cleared of blame, but the city and the courts of Italy continued to talk. The prince was the only living witness, and his word was little esteemed. He was normally no match for Crichton, and his sword was a span shorter than his adversary's. The story went that Crichton, on recognizing his superior, had knelt and proffered his sword by the blade, and that the prince had seized it and run him through. Five years later—such is the consistency of human behavior—the prince and two archers disturbed the amours of the organist of the castle basilica and wounded him. The victim named the archers, and the prince abandoned them to justice.

At any rate, the Admirable Crichton was dead at twenty-two, with his promise unfulfilled. A picture was disseminated, showing him on horseback with a lance in one hand and a book in the other, a posture equally inapt for reading or fighting. The picture, unhappily, has not survived.

Shall we mourn his early disappearance? Various encomia call him the glory and ornament of Parnassus, the phoenix of nature, a shining particle of divine mind and majesty. On the other hand his extant Latin poems offer no great reward. Scaliger says *"Il était un peu fat"* (a bit of a coxcomb); he was more worthy of wonder than of love. The scholar Boccalini asserts that while Crichton astonished the vulgar, he nauseated the wise by his pretensions.

He has left us, at least, an ideal of universal accomplishment, and he has left us a phrase: "the Admirable Crichton." To leave a phrase—that is a rare and splendid legacy.

François de La Rochefoucauld

2 La Rochefoucauld, the Cynical Duke

I mount the steps and ring the bell, turning
Wearily, as one would turn to nod good-bye to Rochefoucauld,
If the street were time and he at the end of the street. . . .

So wrote young T. S. Eliot, weary, disillusioned, walking the sad street of time through the Boston wasteland in company with his disillusioned elder. One may be fairly sure it was drizzling.

Eliot's companion in gloom was the Duc de La Rochefoucauld, seventeenth-century French moralist, soldier, intriguer against the government of Cardinal Richelieu, and lover of three of the most remarkable women of the century: the Duchesse de Chevreuse, the Duchesse de Longueville, and Mme de La Fayette. He is commonly tagged as La Rochefoucauld the Cynic.

What is a cynic like? Do great loves end in cynicism, or does cynicism aid one in becoming a great lover? How does one get to be cynic? Let us examine the case of François de La Rochefoucauld.

He was born in 1613 to greatness, of an ancient and mighty family. His blood was presumed to be of a slightly lighter blue than that of the Princes of the Blood (in those days blood types were distinguished by inherited rank). The marks of his noble caste were pride, honor, courage, courtesy—and cruelty, rapacity, and contempt for common men, which can readily become contempt for all humanity. But some few bear hard the burden of aristocracy. They torture themselves in secret; they question their own eminence.

Young François was shy and sensitive, introspective, a dreamer. The scenery of his land of dreams was provided by the pastoral novels of his time, wherein beribboned shepherds endlessly flute their hopeless love to queenly shepherdesses, inexorably chaste. He knew Honoré d'Urfé's *Astrée* almost by heart, and all his life he read and reread it, even when he became a misanthropic gouty old man. We can no longer dwell in the dreamland of *Astrée*; only one living mortal, to my knowledge, has finished its 5,216 pages.

François was married at fourteen, for financial and dynastic reasons. He went to the wars almost immediately, and within a year was commissioned a colonel, commanding the Auvergne regiment. The realities both of marriage and of war no doubt jarred his dreams of love and heroism.

When that everlasting war, which we call the Thirty Years' War, fell into a lull, François and his bride made their court in Paris. The king, Louis XIII, was a poor creature, with a hundred valet's virtues, people said, and not a single master's virtue. He left all the kingdom's business to his mighty minister, Cardinal Richelieu. His own business, to get the queen a son, he postponed until twenty-two years after his marriage.

The queen was Anne of Austria, daughter of Philip III, king of Spain. She was of her husband's age, and twelve years older than our François. She was tall, very white and blonde, full-figured and full-breasted, and had beautiful hands of which she was very proud. Her inseparable companion was the Duchesse de Chevreuse. The Duchesse possessed "a powerful beauty," records Cardinal Richelieu, who wooed her in vain. Others were more fortunate, at least in a way. She was forever organizing conspiracies against the government, with her lovers as leaders. The conspiracies were always discovered and the leaders either jailed or executed. People compared her to the horse of Sejus, which carried all its riders to disaster.

François adored and pitied the lovely, neglected queen. He was admitted to her intimacy and (it is universally presumed) to the alarming favors of the Duchesse de Chevreuse. He made dizzy plans to abduct the queen, to carry her off to Belgium. He was involved in the machinations of the Duchesse. When she was banished to a château in Touraine, he served as courier between her and the queen, bearing innocent-looking letters with treason between the lines in invisible ink.

It was arranged, during a certain crisis, that the queen should warn Mme de Chevreuse if an order were issued for her imprisonment. If the queen should succeed in allaying suspicion, she would send her friend a Book of Hours bound in green. But if all were lost, she would send a red-bound book, and Mme de Chevreuse must immediately flee the kingdom.

At the height of the crisis the queen was rudely interrogated by Richelieu, but she faced down her inquisitor and kept her friend's secrets intact. She ordered a faithful maid of honor to send the Duchesse a Book of Hours symbolically bound. Green, stay quiet; red, escape. But wait a bit; was it not the other way round? Repeat it a dozen times and the words become a colored blur. At any rate, the queen or the maid of honor or Mme de Chevreuse made a mistake, and the recipient took the message to be: Flee for your life!

The Duchesse rubbed her face with soot and brick dust, donned a male blond wig and a musketeer's jacket, breeches, and jack boots, and set forth with two menservants for the Spanish border. They galloped ninety-two miles in twelve hours, to Ruffec, between Poitiers and Angoulême. The horses were done in, and the Duchesse's tender flesh, unused to the chafe of breeches, bloodied the saddle.

Now François was in his château at Verteuil, only three miles from Ruffec. When he received the Duchesse's message that she was at hand, his first impulse was to conduct her into Spain himself. Then he thought better of it and sent his coach, horses, and manservant instead. After many splendid adventures, she got safely over the Pyrenees, only to find that she might better have stayed at home.

This episode marks a stage in La Rochefoucauld's development. He acted sensibly, prudently; but prudence, he later reflected, can never assure us of success. Céladon, the hero of *Astrée*, would not have been prudent; he would have sprung to his lady's side. The world is teaching La Rochefoucauld, giving him lessons in its meaner values, lessons in the avoidance of folly. But, as he himself was later to say, whoever lives without folly is not so wise as he thinks.

Richelieu died in December, 1642, and the king five months later. The queen began to rule as regent for her four-year-old son, Louis XIV. All the malcontents hurried to court to receive rewards for their fidelity to the queen. But fidelity is a ware that depreciates with time, as La Rochefoucauld himself might have remarked. The way to the queen was barred by her counselor, Cardinal Mazarin, a supple, oily Sicilian nobody. He was probably the queen's lover and possibly her husband (for, though a cardinal, he was not a priest).

The nobles, disappointed in their vision of high posts, grants, and honors, broke up into factions, hostile to Mazarin and to each other. The women were in the thick of the intrigues, for in France politics and love have always been the best of bedfellows.

La Rochefoucauld threw in his lot with the party of the Prince de Condé, a Prince of the Blood, a cousin of the king. For advantage, or at least partly for advantage, he proposed to seduce Condé's sister, the Duchesse de Longueville. She was very beautiful, tall, with turquoise eyes and delicate ash-blonde hair framing her face in rippling curls. Her air of indolence disguised her steely purpose—to exalt her house and herself—

while her freedoms disguised an inward austerity. At her first ball she had worn a hair shirt under her bodice; in her old age she retreated into a morose Jansenism. She was an extraordinary woman in a world of extraordinary women. La Rochefoucauld made her his conquest; and, as so often, he himself fell subject to the conquered. *Vae victis*, to be sure, but also *vae victoribus*.

There is no question that he loved the Duchesse de Longueville, his Anne-Geneviève, ardently, devotedly, knowing the range of love from joy to agony. Later he could look back cynically, for, as he says, there are very few who, having once ceased to love, are not ashamed of having loved. His disappointments, his failures, even his successes, led him further along the road of disillusion.

He served his love and his lady's family interests through the Wars of the Fronde. These were three civil wars lasting from 1648 to 1652. They represented the last organized effort of the French nobles and the bourgeoisie to gain power at the expense of the monarchy. They are immensely confused and confusing, with a half-dozen parties in the field, with constant defections from one side to another as leaders yielded to the temptations of money, pride, and love. All were pursuing self-interest, but it was seldom quite clear, even to them, where their interests lay.

The Fronde was rich in picturesque incident. At the beginning of 1649, the Duchesse de Longueville's party was wooing the somewhat reluctant burghers of Paris. She conceived a master stroke. Big with La Rochefoucauld's child, she chose to spend her confinement in the bourgeois center, the Hôtel de Ville. She triumphantly produced a son, who spent a good portion of his first hours being held up to the window. He was named Charles-Paris by his godfather, the Provost of Paris Merchants. (But the child's father had to stand in the background and crane his neck in order to see the christening of his son.) The sentimental heart of Paris was deeply moved, while the Duchesse continued to intrigue from her bed.

There was another wonderful scene involving La Roche-foucauld, in the Palais de Justice, where the Parlement met. Two parties were at odds—that of Bishop Coadjutor de Retz, a pistol-packing prelate, later cardinal, and that of the Prince de Condé, seconded by our La Rochefoucauld. Retz's gentlemen held the doorways and stairheads; against them La Rochefoucauld disposed his men strategically. As the Councilors of the Parlement trembled under their ermine-furred red robes, Condé and Retz defied each other. Swords flashed out and the President of the Parlement ordered the great hall cleared. The rival leaders bowed. In a confused movement Retz took alarm at a cluster of enemies; he moved to join his men in an adjacent chamber. But let La Rochefoucauld tell his own story:

"At his [the Bishop Coadjutor's] sight the men of his party drew their swords without knowing the reason, and the friends of Monsieur le Prince did the same. Everyone ranged himself according to the party he served, and in a moment the two bands were separated only by the length of their swords, although not one made a thrust or discharged a pistol. The Coadjutor, seeing so much disorder, recognized his peril, and to escape it tried to return to the great hall; but on arriving at the door of the hall by which he had emerged, he found that I had taken possession of it. He tried hard to open it, but as only one side of it opened and this I held, I shut it on the Coadjutor as he was re-entering in such a way that it caught him with his head on the side of the Ushers' Chamber and his body in the great hall."

Thus La Rochefoucauld held the great double door, with Retz's distorted face pilloried a few inches from his own. He fastened the catch which held the two halves of the door ajar and shouted to his partisans beyond the door to reach for their daggers and stab the bishop while he was held fast. However, no one quite liked to be the first to stab his bishop in the back. The gentlemen looked to Condé for orders; he gave no sign. A member of the Parlement cast his cloak about Retz. Another pounced on La Rochefoucauld from behind. Retz was released and orders were shouted to sheathe all swords. Retz faced about and humbly begged the Parlement's pardon for the scandalous scene provoked by his enemies. All the honors of the engagement were his. As he swept out of the hall La Rochefoucauld was seething with anger and ready to challenge him to a duel. "Be calm, my friend *La Franchise*," called out Retz in carrying tones. "You are a coward and I am a priest. There will be no duel between us."

La Rochefoucauld had made a spiritual as well as a tactical fault. He had misjudged others' minds; in his excitement he had not sensed his fellows' reluctance to assassinate a pinioned prelate. He had not been knightly; he had been grotesque, as the very position of his intended victim was grotesque. He had been ridiculous; and, as he says, ridiculousness dishonors more than does dishonor.

The Fronde ended with the Battle of the Faubourg Saint-Antoine, when Condé stormed in vain the walls of Paris. La Rochefoucauld fought savagely until he was hit full in the face by a musket bullet, which nearly blinded him. Condé retreated and soon took service with Spain to fight against his fatherland. The Duchesse de Longueville was driven back to her husband, to live with him in mutual hate and sullen lethargy. La Rochefoucauld was rusticated to his château at Verteuil. He had lost nearly everything: most of his property and most of his eyesight, the Duchesse de Longueville, his self-esteem, the esteem of others, and his esteem of them.

Brooding over his disappointments, he wrote his memoirs. They are a justification of his conduct, of course, but as he wrote he was forced to reflect on the justification of his justifications. Though we admit our faults, he says, we are not entirely frank. We admit them in order to repair by our sincerity the harm they do us in other men's minds. But sincerity is no easy matter, for in a large measure, it consists of our desire to talk about ourselves and to display our defects in the way we want to present them. And the fact is we would rather say evil about ourselves than not talk of ourselves at all.

He had lived in a noble world of falsity. Though he had seen outward evidence of virtue, fidelity, courage, and generosity, mostly he had seen vanity, avarice, folly, futility, and weakness. And even virtue is seldom pure: "Virtue would not go far if vanity did not keep it company." Our souls are stained; they are defective from birth. "The defects of the soul are like the body's wounds; whatever care we may take to cure them, the scar remains forever, and they are always in danger of opening again." There is not much use talking of our qualities of spirit; they are commanded by circumstances, by the body. "Strength and weakness of mind are ill named. They are in fact only the good or evil disposition of the body's organs."

Looking into his own character, he recognized, as did Retz and other acute observers, his disastrous flaw: a paralyzing irresolution. He thought too much; he could see too many sides of a question. He did not possess the happy motor reflexes of the man of action. In a pinch, as in the scene of the bishop's entrapment in the Palais de Justice doors, he dared to follow his impulse, and his impulse betrayed him. He was not made to rule; he was made to look at the world and at himself, and to find his own little parcel of truth.

A few years later he began to venture back to Paris for long visits. Gouty and half-blind, he seemed harmless to Cardinal Mazarin, who was then comfortable in the seat of power. The court was barred to La Rochefoucauld, but he had no desire to resume the wearisome trade of the courtier. "One is nearly always bored in the presence of people with whom it is not permitted to be bored."

He was far happier in the literary salons of Paris. Of these the most congenial was that of Mme de Sablé. She had been amorous in youth, but time had brought repentance. (Or, as La Rochefoucauld put it, "when vices quit us, we flatter ourselves with the belief that it is we who are quitting them.") She became a fervent Jansenist without losing her passion for literature and for *la haute cuisine*. She was plump, pink, and overfed ("a fat turkey," said a contemporary), and she lived in perpetual terror of infection. She bought a house adjoining the Jansenist headquarters of Port-Royal de Paris, made a private bridge to the upper level of the convent chapel, and built there a tiny tribune where she could hear mass without fear of contagion from the holy but unsanitary nuns. She compounded her own remedies, including powdered viper, which La Rochefoucauld found excellent. He applauded also her soups, jams, and marmalades. He brooded over a dinner whereat she had served a *potage aux carottes*, a *ragoût de mouton*, and a *chapon aux pruneaux;* he asked for her recipes for *eau de noix* and for *mille-fleurs*. Well, when love and ambition are at an end, a stout stomach is our best friend.

Mme de Sablé's salon was a peerless assembly of noble bluestockings, including the Duchesse de Longueville, and of men of letters, of whom the greatest was the great Pascal. One had to pass a summary medical inspection by the porter at her door, who intrepidly excluded any cougher or sniffler. Within reigned a high intellectual tone, with special concern for the resolution of moral problems. A favorite game was the confection of maxims. An habitué would present an observation on human behavior in epigrammatic form. The others would first applaud and then criticize, questioning the maxim's truth and novelty, suggesting alternative phrasings, working and reworking the thought for sharpness and concision. But let us postpone for a moment the examination of the maxims.

A first authorized edition of La Rochefoucauld's *Réflexions, ou sentences et maximes morales* appeared in 1665. It had a considerable success, of *estime*, *scandale*, and *librairie*. The supreme tribute was paid by dear Mme de La Fayette; its perusal gave her a three-month attack of liver trouble.

Marie-Madeleine Pioche de La Vergne, Comtesse de La Fayette, was a member of the minor nobility, but was related by marriage to greater nobles. She was poor among the rich and had to make her way and establish her two sons by shifts and devices, even by a little mild espionage. (There were so few ways for a lady to make money!) She had had an unusual education for a woman; she was definitely an intellectual and had published a novelette anonymously.

When Mme de La Fayette read La Rochefoucauld's *Maximes* she wrote to Mme de Sablé, "Ah, Madame, what corruption one must have in mind and heart to be able to imagine all that!" Despite her touch of liver, she conceived a mission: to prove to this disillusioned cynic that a really good woman could support every trial of ill health and ill fortune and retain her reasoned faith in goodness and virtue.

Goodness and virtue do not exclude astuteness. Mme de La Fayette made friends with the son of La Rochefoucauld and the Duchesse de Longueville, now a handsome youth of sixteen. She used him as a lure to draw his father to her little house. Before long the Duc de La Rochefoucauld found himself comfortably installed in an easy chair by Mme de La Fayette's hearth fire. It was discovered that both loved, a little ashamedly, the pastoral novel *Astrée*. During endless happy hours she would read aloud the interminable adventures of the sighing swains and timorous, obdurate nymphs. It is a curious picture of the intimate life of a cynic, as though H. L. Mencken were to solace himself with *Little Women*.

The two gave themselves to literature. Mme de La Fayette produced, among several novels, *La Princesse de Clèves*, the first realistic psychological novel in French, the ancestor of perhaps half a million others. It is still required reading in every survey course in French literature. La Rochefoucauld had a share in it, though no one knows how far the collaboration extended. A contemporary lady wrote: "M. de La Rochefoucauld and Mme de La Fayette have done a novel on the gallantries of the court of Henri II which is said to be admirably well written. They are no longer of an age to do anything else together."

Few know how to be old, La Rochefoucauld confessed. He was ridden by gout, tortured by ennui. He sought strange diversions, such as raising white mice in cages. He remarked that one of the greatest secrets of life is to know how to be bored, for boredom, if pushed to a certain point, serves to distract us. The best of his diversions was the composition and revision of his *Maximes*. He was amused by playing the role of moralist. Old men, he said, love to give good precepts, to console themselves for being no longer in a position to give bad examples.

He died, with relief, in 1680, at the age of sixty-six.

A maxim is an observation on behavior, abstracted and generalized, laid to the account of humanity at large and expressed with the utmost concision. A perfect maxim is compounded with careful art; it requires a discovery of the only exact words, and sound structure of thought, and verbal harmony, rhythm, and balance. Its brevity is the product of long labor. It is the great achievement of the literary miniaturist.

Let us take as an example: the maxim just quoted: "Old men love to give good precepts, to console themselves for being no longer in a position to give bad examples"—"*Les vieillards aiment à donner de bons préceptes, pour se consoler de n'être plus en état de donner de mauvais exemples.*" The starting point was no doubt an observed fact. Perhaps Cardinal de Retz, who came occasionally to gossip with his old enemy, pronounced himself sagely and La Rochefoucauld was reminded of the evil examples lavished by Retz as a dissolute bishop coadjutor. Or perhaps he needed only to reflect on the discord between his own wise words and his youthful folly. His new-found wisdom, he thought, was not the product of moral elevation but of physiology. The breakdown of the tissues fortifies our high principles; our thought hardens with our arteries. He generalizes the statement; not "Naughty old Retz is always laying down the law," not "I find myself, strangely, giving moral lessons," but "Old men love to give. . . ." Love to give what? Tenets, dogmas, maxims, propositions, doctrines, formulas, principles, advice, counsel, recommendations, admonitions, injunctions, directions? On the whole, "precepts," both for sense and sound. Put in two emotion verbs, "love" and "console." Balance the two parts of the sentence, but not too obviously. The first part is (in French) a perfect twelve syllable Alexandrine with a feminine ending. Can we shorten the second part to read: "to console themselves for no longer giving bad examples"? No; the thought would not be complete. Shall the translator say "no longer being" or "being no longer"? I think "being no longer" makes a better rhythm. Each of the maxim's phrases concludes with the essential word: "precepts, examples." There is a fine bang at the end; the point of the whole is clear only with the last word.

Though the genesis of a maxim is regularly an observation of life, the development may vary widely. Some of La Rochefoucauld's observations turn into mere witty sallies, plays on words. Others are casts at clouded truth. And some rise to become revelations of our spirits and our fate.

Here are some to be classified as witty sallies, *boutades:* "Why do we have enough memory to recall the smallest details of what has happened to us, and not enough to remember how many times we have told them to the same person?" Or this: "The reason that lovers and their ladies are not bored at being together is that they are always talking of themselves." Or this eleven-word capsule: "The refusal of praise is a desire to be praised twice." Or finally: "In first passions, women love the lover; in later ones they love love." This is essentially verbalism, enforced by the repetition of significant syllables: *aiment-amant-aiment-amour*. But it is of course something more. It may even be a truth.

Here are some casts at clouded truths. "We are never so happy or so unhappy as we imagine." We can expand it to read: "The fantasies of the mind dominate what we fondly call our emotions. We are proud of our capacity for feeling; we like to think of our vast despairs, our blinding bliss; thus we make ourselves interesting to ourselves and to others. But in truth we are incapable of such frenzies; we are sluggish self-deceivers. Our great emotions are falsities, self-deceptions, pitiful glorifications of our inadequate ability to feel." One may expand further to make an entire novel. But it is all there, again in eleven words: "We are never so happy or so unhappy as we imagine."

"It is more shameful to distrust one's friends than to be deceived by them." Then true friendship exists; it is noble; it does not admit the possibility of deception. The way of honor is to be true to friendship, even if friendship should cheat. The maxim is not cynical at all; it is the expression of a high ideal.

"Most men's gratitude is merely a secret desire to receive greater benefits." "Our envy always lasts longer than the good fortune of those we envy." "Hypocrisy is an homage that vice renders to virtue." "In the adversity of our best friends we always find something that does not entirely displease us." Are these allegations true? They are challenges; we must test them and accept or reject them according to our experience of ourselves and of the world.

And some of the maxims are more than challenges; they are revelations, telling us something we had not known or had not realized. "Folly pursues us at all stages of life. If a man seems wise, it is merely because his follies are suited to his age and fortune." "Jealousy is always born with love, but does not always die with it." And these penetrating words: "Weak people cannot be sincere."

I sit quiet and pretend I am La Rochefoucauld. I try to assemble my experience of life. *Experientia docet*, they say—experience teaches. No doubt; but what exactly has it taught? I am nonplused; I perceive no lesson ready to hand. But I perceive the glimmer of a maxim: "Experience teaches; we cannot remember just what." Perhaps I too can play La Rochefoucauld's game.

Asking myself what in fact experience has taught, I cast my mind backward. Memory presents me with a boy's distressful wonder about whether he really exists in a real world, or if he is an illusion within an illusion. I recall youth's dreadful, clumsy experiments, its plunges into danger and folly, its escapes, maimed and lacerated. And I pronounce: "Many a man has lost his life to prove to himself that he existed."

I have not produced maxims worthy of La Rochefoucauld, but I think I have penetrated somewhat his mind and explored somewhat the heart of a cynic. La Rochefoucauld's work is commonly taken as the expression of mocking disillusion. It is that, of course, but it is something more. For one who has lived in illusion, disillusion is an agony. La Rochefoucauld's maxims are not perverse reversals of accepted values, done by formula, nor are they abstract generalizations on human behavior. They are confessions; they are recognitions of an idealist's defeat by the world. They are the list of injuries done to his ideal. They are a cry of pain that the world is what it is.

The heart of a cynic is a broken heart.

Constant Phaulkon, hatless and on all fours, urges the French ambassador to raise up the letter from Louis XIV, while the King of Siam graciously stoops to take it

3 The Tragedy of Constant Phaulkon

In 1648 or thereabouts the great lottery of fate tossed a winning number to the Greek island of Cephalonia. It fell in the cradle of Kostantinos Gerakis, a poor tavern-keeper's son. "Gerakis" means "Falcon"; the surname fitted the recipient better than do most. Later he found it convenient to translate the name into Western form, and thus history remembers him, though with an effort, as Constant Phaulkon.

When he was about twelve he shipped as cabin boy aboard an English trading vessel. A likely lad, he learned seamanship and fluent English and the arithmetic of profit and loss. He joined the Church of England, no doubt more from policy than conviction. When about twenty-two, he went out to the East as cabin boy on an East Indiaman and attracted the favorable notice of the supercargo (or captain?), George White. He and White deserted the East India Company and traded independently, as "interlopers," from the Persian Gulf to Indonesia. Phaulkon, who had already picked up Portuguese and Malay on his travels, added Siamese to his linguistic stock and made many valuable business contacts.

He now bought a half-interest in the sloop *Mary*, and acting as master, set off on a trading trip to Sumatra. But he wrecked the *Mary* somewhere on the way. He met on the shore the Siamese ambassador to Persia, likewise shipwrecked, whom he brought safely back to Siam in a small boat, and was rewarded by introductions and recommendations to the barcalon, or prime minister, and other high officials.

The story has a rather fabulous sound, but the *Mary* was certainly wrecked, and Phaulkon certainly appeared soon after as the controller of commerce for the kingdom of Siam. He had recognized and seized that opportunity of which every ambitious man dreams. The door to power briefly opened before him, and he boldly entered.

The circumstances were propitious. The king of Siam, Narai, an intelligent and genial monarch, held the monopoly of his country's foreign trade. Operations were in the hands of Mohammedan Indonesians working with the Dutch merchant fleet. Their graft was monumental and was undisturbed by the Siamese ministers, sunk in pride and sloth. When Phaulkon was appointed Chief Merchant, he arrested and tortured the leading Indonesians and suppressed all speculations except, of course, his own. The king, in gratitude, made him a high-class mandarin and conferred on him a hat hung with bells. The king proposed further to install him as his barcalon. But Phaulkon refused, recognizing the hostility that would ensue and preferring the reality of power to its semblance.

The king was an absolute ruler, whose holiness set him above all ordinary humanity. He dwelt hidden in his palace, only rarely showing his face even to his ministers. But he was bored by his solitary eminence. He made Phaulkon his confidant and companion and could not be parted from him for a day.

Phaulkon repaid the king's favor with genuine devotion. He was a man of great personal charm, lusty and gusty, with an insinuating manner. He held men spellbound with his fiery eyes, wherein lurked something dark and mysterious, and he had a remarkable range of knowledge.

In 1682 he was reconverted to Catholicism, his childhood faith. He proved a zealous Christian, rising at five daily to spend an hour in pious meditation before beginning the day's business. Twice a week he fed the poor, and on Holy Thursdays he washed the feet of twelve beggars and served them dinner, on his knees, to general bewilderment.

Religion was not allowed to interfere with business—quite the reverse, in fact. Siam's foreign trade was restricted by the jealous power of the Dutch East India Company. Phaulkon proposed to combat it by calling in the French. He filled the king's mind with tales of Louis XIV's might and magnificence, and he sent gift-laden ambassadors to the Sun King. They bore letters appealing to Louis' cupidity by promising great returns in trade, and to his piety by hinting that King Narai was ripe for conversion to Catholic Christianity.

King Louis, readily persuaded, sent out an expedition in the spring of 1685 under the command of an ambassador, the Chevalier de Chaumont. He added a number of ecclesiastics, including six learned Jesuits.

After a seven-month voyage, the envoys disembarked in Siam. They were transported up the river Menam in the king's splendid galleys, and in the capital, Ayuthia, were magnificently welcomed by Phaulkon. The letter from Louis to the king of Siam, on its golden salver, was convoyed separately, in a glittering gilded barge.

Here a knotty problem of etiquette presented itself. Ambassador Chaumont wished to hand Louis' letter directly to the king. Phaulkon protested that the ambassador must lie prostrate in the king's presence. After several messages to and fro, permission was granted to the ambassador to stand at the solemn moment. Therefore, at the palace door, the Abbé de Choisy took the letter and placed it on a golden bowl supported by a three-and-a-half-foot staff. Trumpets and drums sounded; Chaumont, Choisy, and Phaulkon marched to the audience chamber between two rows of a thousand soldiers sitting on their heels. The room was filled with prostrate mandarins, but the envoys saw no king until he showed himself enthroned, peering out through a small window some six feet above the ground. The mandarins clasped their hands behind their heads and knocked their foreheads resoundingly on the floor. Phaulkon removed his slippers and crawled on all fours toward the window. Chaumont doffed his hat and made three obeisances in the French style. He then read a very ill-timed address summoning Narai to join the Roman Catholic Church. Fortunately only the French understood it.

Now came the holy moment of the presentation of Louis' letter. Chaumont took the golden bowl in his hand. To reach Narai he would have to hold the staff at its base and raise the bowl high. This action, he felt, was beneath the dignity of France; he would bend his elbow, not raise his arm from the shoulder. Phaulkon, crouching on the floor, cried in agony: "Higher! Higher!" But the king, smiling at barbarian punctilio, graciously leaned down from his window, took the letter, and placed it on his head. A great sigh of relief filled the chamber.

Chaumont and the other French envoys had several further audiences with the king. Chaumont, a recent and zealous convert from Protestantism, dwelt forever on the proofs of Catholicism. The king was bored; he had expected business deals and an alliance against the Dutch. He said, with Buddhist tolerance, that all religions are true and all are imposed by God to meet the needs of diverse nations.

However, the visitors were more than royally entertained. They inspected the famous white elephant, fed only from gold vessels and attended by four mandarins, who fanned him and shaded his eyes with parasols. Phaulkon took them on hunts, guiding his own elephant, a sports model, at a spirited trot. He treated them to magnificent festivities that included fireworks, jugglers, and tumblers, and a very long and tiresome Chinese opera.

The diplomatic mission was counted a success by both parties. Two years later Louis XIV sent out a military-religious mission with fourteen Jesuits, 636 officers and soldiers, and magnificent presents and kindly letters to the king and to Phaulkon.

Meanwhile, however, Phaulkon's standing deteriorated. He weathered a rebellion prompted by the Indonesians and Malays, but his enemies were gaining strength. And the king was ill from a gathering dropsy.

Now in 1688, a Siamese strong man, P'ra P'et Rāchā, Keeper of the Royal Elephants, mounted a full-scale rebellion. Phaulkon scorned the advice of the French that he abdicate his post and flee to France. The French commander refused to commit his troops. P'ra P'et Rāchā invaded the royal palace and seized Phaulkon and the dying king. The king's two younger brothers were respectfully inserted into sacks of scarlet velvet and pounded to death with sandalwood clubs, "which is in Siam a torture reserved for persons of the highest consideration." The heir to the throne, Narai's adopted son, was beheaded. Phaulkon was led to the execution place in the forest. He knelt, prayed, and protested his innocence of imputed crimes. He was then beheaded by a backhand saber-blow, according to Siamese ritual.

Shortly afterward the king died and was succeeded by P'ra P'et Rāchā. The French sailed away. An antiforeign and anti-Christian spirit possessed the country, and Siam remained off limits to Western traders for a century and a half.

And what of the great Phaulkon, who died at forty, after rising from cabin boy to effective ruler of a kingdom? Does he inform us at all of the human spirit, the human lot? His contemporaries applaud his intelligence, his quick wit, his decision, his courage, his impatience with verbiage and circumlocution, his "magnificence," or lavishness, his charm, and his apparently genuine piety. Turning the coin, they reprove his pride, cruelty, violence of temper, greed for honors, if not money, and his vanity and unappeasable ambition. But a man is more than a sum of qualities; he is an indivisible entity. One who knew him speaks of his "indescribable air of authority."

This, I think, is the clue. The dominant man, the great man, in government, business, all human relations, possesses the indescribable air of authority. This comes from within; it cannot be learned or taught. It expresses a quality of spirit beyond our definition. He who owns it is driven to mastery despite himself, and in the end he is likely to be undone by fate's backhand saber-blow, representing the victory of the commonplace over the exceptional. This is a favorite theme of ancient Greek tragedy; and Phaulkon's story is a modern Greek tragedy.

A short-lived experiment in piratical democracy on the island of Madagascar

A Captain Tew
on the
Grand Account

In the month of October, 1694, His Excellency Governor Benjamin Fletcher of His Majesty's Province of New York was frequently noticed, on his progresses through the city in his six-horse coach, in company with a slight, dark man of forty, dressed with finicking elegance. The governor's guest wore a blue jacket bordered with gold lace, short trousers of white linen covering his legs to the knee, and embroidered stockings. Around his neck was a chain of beaten gold and in his belt a dagger, the hilt set with jewels in Orient style. The burghers nodded slyly and made little jokes in Dutch. They recognized Thomas Tew, a Red Sea man, a rambler, an expeditioner on the grand account, or, to make short of it, a pirate.

Captain Tew was treated by his host with every consideration, nay even affection. He was bidden to the governor's table, where, it appears, he behaved with indecent jollity, unreprimanded. The governor, being later reproached for this familiarity, wrote to the Council for Trade and Plantations: "This Tew appeared to me not only a man of courage and activity, but of the greatest sense and remembrance of what he had seen, of any seaman I had mett. He was allso what they call a very

41

pleasant man; soe that at times when the labours of my day were over it was some divertisment as well as information to me, to heare him talke. I wish'd in my mind to make him a sober man, and in particular to reclaim him from a vile habit of swearing. I gave him a booke to that purpose; and to gaine the more upon him, I gave him a gunn of some value. In returne hereof he made me also a present which was a curiosity and in value not much; and this is the sum of all that kindness I am charged with; for as to the coming sometimes to my table, which I think was such as became my character, and hospitable to all, I hope that will not stick upon me."

The governor, a godly man and the first founder of New York's Trinity Church, learned that the censorious will besmirch the purest motives. Four years later an investigator asserted to the Council for Trade that Tew and a piratical companion named Hore were known to be of no morals, but of the most dissolute principles, as well as of lewd and infamous behavior. It was generally reported, said he, that to Colonel Fletcher's own knowledge and in his own company they had violated the laws of God and man by drunkenness, blasphemy, and swearing. Hore, especially, was said to have committed excesses of debauchery in the Government House—although, unfortunately, no details of his behavior have been preserved.

We are led to believe, however, that as Red Sea songs sounded from the Government House, and as the government wine glasses were merrily shivered, the solid citizens of New York echoed the official glee. For the merchants were deeply implicated in the outfitting of pirates and in the purchase of their spoils. Four ships that had been on the grand account entered the harbor one summer with cargoes estimated at from £50,000 to £300,000. New York was filled with Oriental rugs, teakwood furniture, metal wares, and stuffs from India's looms. Arabian gold was common and passed readily at a fixed rate in dollars.

The chief entrepreneur in the Red Sea trade was Frederick Philipse, whose Manor Hall in Yonkers is still held in reverence. His practice was to send forth ships laden with weapons, ammunition, and liquor, consigned to some innocuous destination. Capricious winds would bring them to Madagascar, the pirate headquarters. In time his bottoms would return with Oriental goods acquired by blameless purchase.

The profits of such commerce were great. Captain Giles Shelly, who was in the Madagascar trade, bought rum for 2 shillings per gallon in New York and sold it to the parched pirates for £3; he sold a £19 pipe of Madeira for £300. And the advantage on his return cargo was no less interesting.

Governor Fletcher looked upon this fruitful business with much benevolence. To sea captains who were properly presented he would give privateering commissions to war against the French. As he later protested to his Lords of Trade, he could hardly be held responsible if the privateers crossed the dim line dividing their duty from piracy.

Such a commission was granted to Captain Tew, requiring him, out of caution, to sign a bond of £3,000 for his good behavior. The governor's fee was said to be £300. The bond was guaranteed by Edward Coates, a conspicuous pirate, who sent Madame Fletcher a present of jewels, silks, and cashmere shawls. Coates's liberality was indeed notorious; his gifts to men in place and their dear ones amounted to £1,800.

This Thomas Tew was a Rhode Island boy, the scion of a good Newport family. The record of his early years has not been preserved, but in 1691 he appeared in Bermuda and made it no secret that he had already been rambling and would gladly ramble again. Bermuda merchants and the governor of the island took shares with him in a sloop of 70 tons burthen, whimsically named the *Amity*, with a complement of sixty men and eight guns. He sailed with a commission in pocket to capture a

French factory on the Guinea coast.

In African waters, he assembled his crew, and, according to the spirited contemporary record of Captain Charles Johnson, addressed them in this tenor: that he thought the attack on the French factory a very injudicious expedition which, even if successful, would be of no use to the public, and only advantage a private company of men from whom they could expect no reward of their bravery; that he could see nothing but danger in the undertaking, without the least prospect of booty; that he could not suppose any man fond of fighting for fighting's sake, for few ventured their lives but with some view either of particular interest or public good, and that here was not the least appearance of either. Wherefore, he was of the opinion that they should turn their thoughts to what might better their circumstances, and if they were so inclined, he would undertake to shape a course that should lead them to ease and plenty in which they might pass the rest of their days. One bold push would do their business, and they might return home, not only without danger but even with reputation.

The crew cried out, one and all: "A gold chain, or a wooden leg! We'll stand by you!" The men then elected a quartermaster, for pirate ships are democratically governed, and all the captain's proposals must be ratified by the quartermaster. The *Amity* altered her course, rounded the Cape of Good Hope, and came to the Red Sea. There she took a tall ship bound from the Indies for Arabia. The booty was estimated to be between £1,200 and £3,000 per man.

The succession of events is not here perfectly plain. It seems that the *Amity* then returned to Newport. Captain Tew honorably informed his Bermuda partners of his arrival. Their agent found part of their share buried in Newport, part in Boston. One owner received £3,000. Tew's share was £8,000. Lyons dollars and Arabian gold became familiar currency in Rhode Island.

But Captain Tew found life in the prim city humdrum; he was not yet of an age for retirement. He obtained a privateer's commission from the Rhode Island governor for a fee of £500. He visited New York and received the aid of Frederick Philipse in outfitting the *Amity*. This must have occurred in the year 1692.

Tew made an uneventful journey to Madagascar. Off that island, he raised a pair of large ships. Tew threw out his black colors and fired a shot to windward. The stranger fired a shot to leeward and hoisted out a boat, which signified a desire for parley. Tew received an envoy, who announced, betwixt courtesy and laughter, that he was the lieutenant of Captain Misson, famed in the pirate world. He proposed that Tew join his own master, and in the end Tew accepted.

Captain Misson is one of the most winning figures in the annals of piracy. The son of an ancient family of Provence, he was bred to the sea. On a visit to Rome, he conceived doubts of the validity of Catholic dogma. He took his misgivings to the confessional, but fate sent him the most regrettable of confessors, who, far from removing his doubts, suggested a swarm of new ones. On learning that his penitent was a sailor, this sad priest, whose name was Caraccioli, avowed that he had himself always longed for the sea's freedom. Indeed he followed Misson back to his ship and signed on as a recruit, sending his black frock overside. Ere long this renegade made a perfect deist of Misson, representing to him that God has given us the blessing of reason to make use of for our present and future happiness, and whatever is contrary to it must be false.

When Misson captained his own ship, Caraccioli became his mate. On a voyage to the West Indies, they decided to cast in for the grand account. Caraccioli harangued the crew, presenting arguments against both religion and government, maintaining that every man is born free and has as much right to what will support him as to the air he respires.

The crew was readily persuaded and shouted: "*Vive le capitaine Misson et son lieutenant le savant Caraccioli!*" They took many profitable prizes in the West and East Indies, but always with a statement of their high moral purpose. They would have nothing to do with the black flag, for Caraccioli insisted that they were not pirates, but men who were resolved to assert that liberty which God and Nature had given them. He advised therefore a white ensign, with Liberty painted in the fly, and the motto *A Deo a Libertate* (By God and Liberty) as an emblem of their uprightness and resolution.

The ship, *La Victoire*, became a model commonwealth. Misson regarded himself as the father of his men, administering equal and impartial justice. All goods were held in common; no particular avarice was permitted to defraud the public. The captain recommended to his men a brotherly love toward each other, the banishment of all private piques and grudges, and a strict agreement and harmony among themselves. "In throwing off the yoke of tyranny," he exclaimed, "I hope none will follow the example of the tyrants, and turn his back upon justice; for when equity is trodded underfoot, misery, confusion, and mutual distrust naturally follow." It was true, he admitted, that men born and bred in slavery, who dance to the music of their chains, would brand this generous crew with the invidious name of pirates and think it meritorious to be instrumental in their destruction. Self-preservation, therefore, obliged him to declare war against all who should not immediately surrender and give up what their necessities required.

Captain Misson's conduct was constantly in accord with his elevated principles. He set free all the Negroes captured on British slavers, for, he said, the trading for those of our own species can never be agreeable to the eyes of divine justice. He preserved the greatest decorum and regularity on board his ship. Believing his men to have been contaminated by certain Dutch recruits, he preached to his crew, telling them that before the Dutchmen came on board, his ears had never been grated by hearing the name of the great Creator profaned, though, to his sorrow, he had often since heard his own men guilty of that sin. Alcohol, too, had degenerated them into brutes by drowning the only faculty distinguishing man from beast: reason. He gave the Dutch notice that the first man caught either with an oath in his mouth or liquor in his head would be brought to the gears, whipped, and pickled (the piratical practice of lashing a malefactor and rubbing his wounds with salt, pepper, and lemon juice). The Dutch, we are told, grew continent in fear of punishment, as did the French in fear of being reproached by their good captain, "for they never mentioned him without this epithet."

Misson and his men made their headquarters on the island of Johanna, northwest of Madagascar. Misson made a diplomatic marriage with the queen's sister, as did Caraccioli with her niece. After some singular adventures, they removed to Madagascar itself, where they found all the necessities of life: wholesome air, a fruitful soil, and a sea abounding with fish. They chose for their capital the bay of Diego Suarez. Here they founded a thriving city, to which they gave the name of Libertatia. The inhabitants were called *Liberi*, Freemen, and no longer French, British, or Africans. In their well fortified town the Freemen lived in ease and virtue, united in bonds of marriage with the winsome maidens of the happy isle.

These were the high-minded freebooters to whom Captain Tew spoke at sea. Concealing, perhaps, his own faults of profanity and dram drinking, Tew made a good impression on the Freemen. He and his men were made citizens of Libertatia, and did their part in the fortification of the city and in the building of two 80-ton sloops. Tew, who is known in Madagascan history as Tanö, received a noble wife, a princess of the Zafindramisoa family. Their son, the Malată Ratsimilahŏ, was the founder of the kingdom of Betsimarahä.

Tew and Misson made a successful cruise to the Red Sea, where they took a ship belonging to the Great Mogul, bound for Jedda with pilgrims to Mecca. They set the men ashore, but, against the single vote of Captain Misson, carried a hundred girls, between twelve and eighteen years old, to Libertatia.

The constitution and laws of the little state, based on the soundest principles of democracy, should be of the utmost interest to political scientists, who have, however, vouchsafed it little regard. Let it suffice that Misson was elected conservator for a three-year term and the eloquent Caraccioli secretary of state, while our Captain Tew was elevated to the dignity of admiral.

But this experiment in communal government came to a sad end. Admiral Tew, on a cruise in the business way, lost the *Victoire* in a hurricane and barely escaped with his life. During his absence the Madagascar natives descended on the weakened colony and made a dreadful slaughter. Caraccioli died in action, but Misson escaped with the *Amity* and another sloop. Tew rejoined him and proposed that they should go to America, where they might pass their lives in a comfortable manner. But on the way, Misson's sloop went down in a storm, and America was deprived of his experience of a moral republican polity.

Tew shaped his course for home and arrived at Rhode Island without accident. Even after all his disasters, his share and his owners', as he told a friend, amounted to more than £12,000, while his men received more than £1,000 each. Such petty sums were soon spent, however, and the merry companions importuned Tew to make one more cruise. He was not loath to do so; he was irked by Newport's chill decorum. He made application to the new governor, John Easton, for a privateer's commission, apparently indispensable to the pirate. "I know not your design," said Governor Easton. To this Tew answered: "I shall go where perhaps the commission may never be seen or heard of." A commission on such terms was refused by the upright Governor Easton.

And thus we have found Captain Tew in New York in 1694, riding with Governor Fletcher in his carriage, enthralling His Excellency—with how much reason!—with tales of carnage, adventure, practical communism, and love in far tropic islands. How gladly would the present writer exchange the governor's official documents for his private notes of Captain Tew's conversation!

At any rate, Tew received his privateer's commission. He fitted out the *Amity* and two other small vessels in Rhode Island, and made arrangements to meet a ship from Boston and another from a port with the astonishing name of Whoreskill, which was apparently Lewes Creek, in present Delaware. The fleet of five met at a rendezvous in the Liparan Islands, at the mouth of the Red Sea, in June, 1695. Here they engaged a convoy of twenty-five Moors. "In the engagement," says Captain Johnson, "a shot carried away the rim of Tew's belly, who held his bowels with his hands some small space. When he dropped, it struck such terror in his men that they suffered themselves to be taken without making resistance." A deponent heard in Madagascar, not long after, that fourteen of the survivors "had by consent divided themselves into two sevens, to fight for what they had (thinking they had not made a voyage sufficient for so many), and that one of the said sevens were all killed, and five of the other, so that the two which survived enjoyed the whole Booty."

In the end, Governor Fletcher wished that he had never heard Captain Tew's captivating tales. He was recalled to London in a cloud of suspicion, and the Earl of Bellomont was sent out as governor, with orders to suppress the pirate trade.

When Bellomont arrived, he found the city's officials all smiles. The merchants offered him £5,000 and his secretary

£1,000 for protection for an expedition, and he said that in another case he might have received £100,000. He refused all such proffers only to find himself nearly helpless in the hands of the New Yorkers. His Council, mostly merchants interested in the Red Sea trade, contrived to check him at every turn. Those who assisted the governor were terrified by the merchants. His high sheriff was said to have £2,500 in East India goods in his house. The governor's informant refused to testify publicly, for fear of being murdered. In 1698 the *Fortune* (Captain Hore's ship) arrived with a famous cargo. It was secretly put ashore and stowed in the house of Van Sweeten, a merchant of high standing. Bellomont got wind of it and sent his civil officers to seize the goods. But the merchants assembled and locked the officers in the house, whence they were released only by the intervention of Bellomont in person, at the head of all his military.

"They are a wicked and lawlesse people here and very revengefull," wrote the Earl of Bellomont. He found a cure for his troubles, and for those of the New York merchants, by dying, in 1701. His successor, Lord Cornbury, was the one who dressed commonly in women's clothes.

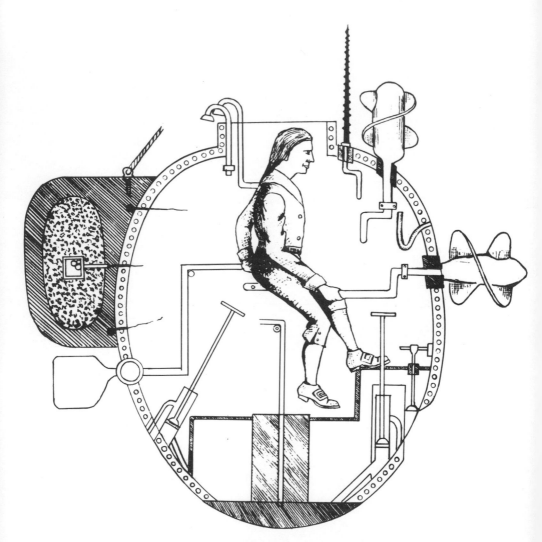

Bushnell's turtle: the first submarine on record

5 David Bushnell
and the
American Turtle

In the late evening of the sixth of September, 1776, General Israel Putnam and a group of Continental officers met on New York's Whitehall wharf, the present South Ferry. They spoke in guarded voices and moved with precaution, for the British slept on Governors Island, half a mile away.

Two whaleboats, rowing cautiously, put in to the wharf. They towed behind them a curious aquatic monster, intended to navigate under water. All that was visible was a squat cylinder, perhaps three feet in diameter and a foot in height, topped by a brass-capped opening and set on rounded shoulders disappearing in the water. Several pipes and shafts bristled from its head.

On the wharf, the inventor of this strange craft, David Bushnell, a slight, nervous young man, explained that he called his contrivance a "torpedo," after the crampfish or electric ray. General Putnam, a foe to such outlandishness, named it merely the Turtle, and by that name it was known to the curious of his time and of times to follow.

David Bushnell insisted, with much deprecation, that only illness and frailty of body prevented him from making personal trial of his submarine vessel. Sergeant Ezra Lee, a vigorous and intrepid youth of Lyme, Connecticut, presented himself as operator.

The brass cap was unscrewed and laid back. Probably some of the engineer officers, but not the portly "Old Put," descended in turn into the machine for an inspection. (It would not accommodate more than one person at a time.) It was shaped like two upper tortoise shells set on end and glued together; the swelling for the animals' heads would represent the entrance. This entrance was kept upright in the water by about seven hundred pounds of lead ballast at the bottom of the shells. Two hundred pounds of this ballast could be dropped forty or fifty feet, to serve as an anchor or to send the machine shooting to the surface. The Turtle measured about six feet in height and seven and a half feet fore and aft. It was built of heavy oak, bound with iron bands, the seams calked, and the whole smeared with tar.

Squeezing through an elliptical opening, the adventurer found himself in a chamber hardly larger than his body. He sat on an oak beam, which served to prevent the shell-shaped walls from collapsing under the pressure of a deep immersion. Handles ringed him round. By turning a crank in front of his stomach, he operated two paddles, twelve inches by four, fixed, like the vanes of a windmill, to an axletree. By vigorous action he could make a speed of three miles an hour. For this, the first screw propeller, Bushnell has not commonly received credit.

A similar propeller, in a shaft ingeniously protected against leakage, protruded upward from the top of the vessel, as on a helicopter, to help in submerging and rising. Astern was a rudder, which could be used both for steering and propulsion. A sounding lead was also carried.

When afloat, the Turtle admitted light through windows in the turret. The operator's eyes, level with these windows, gave him his direction. At night, or under water, he steered by means of a compass treated with fox fire, phosphorescent wood. Air entered through windows, which could be opened in a calm sea, and through a pipe extending upward. The fresh air was carried through this pipe to the bottom of the submarine; naturally rising, it replaced the foul air, which escaped through a second pipe opening by the navigator's head. These air pipes had automatic valves which shut when the water rose near them and opened as the water fell away. When the ship submerged, it contained enough air for thirty minutes' breathing. The increasing foulness would serve the operator, in his dark chamber, as his clock.

To submerge, the operator depressed a valve with his foot; water entered a tank at the bottom of the ship. He regulated his depth by means of a pressure gauge, consisting of a graduated glass tube eighteen inches long, its upper end closed, its lower end communicating with the external water. A phosphorescent cork floated in the gauge, its rise and fall, governed by the pressure of the water outside, indicating how far beneath the surface the submarine was. An inch rise denoted a fathom's submergence. To regain the surface, the operator emptied his tank with two brass forcing pumps, one at each hand.

Such was the first submarine of which we have any record. It was built with a definite purpose: to destroy the British fleet. David Bushnell, first in many things, was the first to demonstrate that gunpowder can be set off under water, and that a submarine charge, lying against a ship, will wreck the ship in its explosion.

His vessel carried on top, behind the hatch, an egg-shaped magazine of oak, containing one hundred and fifty pounds of gunpowder, a clock set to unpinion a gunlock at any given time, and a detonating apparatus. This bomb was to be attached to the bottom of a ship by a large wood screw, set in front of the turret, and turned by a handle within the submarine. The operator's task was to bore a hole in the ship's timber and then to detach the screw, which was bound by a rope to the magazine. This, being lighter than water, should rise against the ship's bottom and bring the enemy to an ingenious doom.

It was about eleven, with the moon yet unrisen and an ebb tide flowing, when the whaleboats left Whitehall with the Turtle in tow. The British fleet was lying in the roadstead north of Staten Island. When the Continentals had rowed as near the sleeping vessels as they dared, Ezra Lee entered his craft. The glimmering windows faced toward the *Eagle*, Admiral Howe's flagship, and with an eerie air of purpose the monster swam away. The whaleboats turned about and pulled back against the current to Manhattan.

The tide was running out, swift and imperious. The men-of-war were dark, and before he knew it, the sergeant found himself in their lee. Recognizing his misfortune, he got his craft about, and by hard labor at the crank for two and a half hours, worked his way back to his prey. In the moonlight he could see men moving on a 50-gun ship, and could hear their conversation. He closed up overhead, let in water, spun his paddles furiously, and soon found himself bumping the ship's bottom. He could not worry about the noise of his collisions; the man-of-war's men, if they thought of it at all, might attribute it to a blundering log.

He groped his way to the flagship's stern, dropped his propeller crank, and seized the handle operating the wood screw. He turned in a kind of void; the screw point would not bite, whether, as Bushnell later explained it, because Lee had struck the iron bar binding the rudder hinge, or, as Lee averred with greater likelihood, because the pressure of the screw merely caused the submarine to rebound, instead of penetrating the sturdy oak of Old England. He attacked several times, after each failure working his way painfully back to his oblivious victim.

Rising to the surface for a fresh supply of air, he found his windows gray. The day was breaking. He dove again, and made a final vain effort to attach his mine. There was nothing more to be done. To delay further would bring only the loss of his machine and all its secrets and all the hopes that it contained.

The tide had turned and was setting northward. He glanced at his compass, to shape his course for the four-mile journey beneath hostile waters. His compass failed him; probably the chilled fox fire had lost its virtue. He was obliged to find his way blindly between the menaces of the enemy above the surface and the bars and eddies below. Grinding wearily at his cranks, he rose at dangerously frequent intervals to take his bearings.

He came to the surface to find himself only a few hundred yards from Governors Island. The British were astir; hundreds of them came running to the parapet, with much shouting, which seemed to signify curiosity rather than fright. A party came down to the beach, manned a barge, and came dipping toward the wide-eyed sea beast.

Lee filled his craft with air, closed his ports, and submerged. One defense remained to him. He reached for the trigger which released his bomb, and set it free, "expecting," says the friend who preserved his story, a certain Dr. Thatcher, "that they would seize that likewise, and thus would be blown to atoms together."

But the British, observing the disappearance of the windowed leviathan, and a strange egg floating on the water, suspected "a Yankee trick." They took alarm and returned to Governors Island, while Sergeant Lee urged his lightened craft with all speed toward Whitehall. Reaching safe waters, he rose and signaled his friends; they put out and rescued him, with what emotions everyone may imagine as he chooses.

The bomb floated idly past Governors Island and into the East River. "In less than half an hour a terrible explosion took place," says Dr. Thacher, who had the story from an eyewitness. "It threw into the air a prodigious column of water, resembling a great water spout, attended with a report like thunder. General Putnam, and others who waited with great anxiety for the result, were exceedingly amused with the astonishment and alarm which this secret explosion occasioned."

Bushnell and his aide would not accept the failure as final. When the Continentals evacuated New York, a few days later, the submarine was taken up the Hudson. An attempt was made by Lee against a frigate lying off Bloomingdale, in the latitude of 106th Street. While trying to fasten his magazine to the ship's stern, close to the water's edge, he was discovered and frightened away by the watch.

This was the end of the experiments and the end of David Bushnell's submarine. In what waters does it tragically lie? In what old shipyard was it left forgotten? Where is the rust of all that ingenuity, all that bold imagination?

David Bushnell was born in Saybrook, Connecticut, about 1742, a farmer's boy. His father died when David was twenty-seven; he immediately sold the farm, prepared for college with the Reverend John Devotion, and entered Yale with the class of 1775. In his freshman year be began to work on his submarine; at some time in his course he demonstrated to the college faculty the explosion of gunpowder under water. "He is no enthusiast; a perfect philosopher," said a friend. Even after the failure of his Turtle, he kept the esteem of his superiors. "I then thought, and still think, that it was an effort of genius," wrote George Washington.

Bushnell abandoned his submarine boat, and sought a simpler way of destroying the enemy's shipping. In August, 1777, he sent a contact mine, floated on a line of buoys, to wrap around, entangle, and destroy the British frigate *Cerberus*, which lay at anchor in Black Point Bay, west of New London. But a schooner intercepted the mine; the curious sailors hauled their prize on board, whereupon it exploded, destroyed the schooner, and killed three men. The captain of the *Cerberus* immediately sailed for New York to warn the fleet against the "secret modes of mischief" of the rebels.

The inventor made one more attempt, less bold, less cunning. When the British men-of-war lay in the Delaware River off Philadelphia, he set adrift, above the city, a squadron of kegs equipped to explode at a touch. The kegs were delayed by a sluggish current; some exploded against cakes of ice, one against a small boat, killing its occupants to vindicate Bushnell's strategy. But the British fleet moved sedately down the river and out of harm's way. This, the renowned Battle of the Kegs, was celebrated in a famous ballad, not without salt, to the tune of "Moggy Lawder."

Bushnell regarded this last miscarriage of his plans as a reproof of fortune. He accepted an appointment in the new corps of sappers and miners, and performed his routine duties in the service of roads and bridges. He fought at Yorktown, and was stationed at West Point until peace came in 1783. He then returned to Connecticut, impoverished, the object of some outward honor, some covert ridicule. In a letter to Thomas Jefferson from Stamford, dated October, 1787, he complains that for two years he has been too ill to reply to Jefferson's request for information.

Here the trace of David Bushnell is for a time obscured. It was rumored that he carried his plans to France. He could have hoped for little success; Robert Fulton, after demonstrating his extraordinary submarine in the harbor of Brest in 1801, was routed by a righteous French admiral: "Thank God, sir, France still fights her battles above the surface and not beneath it!"

Another rumor ran that Bushnell went into some mercantile pursuit abroad which came to disaster. It was said again, but falsely, that he perished in the French Revolution. Finally all rumors ceased about the hearths of Saybrook.

Some time in 1795 or 1796, a furtive visitor, giving the name of Bush, came to the door of Abraham Baldwin, Yale '72, an eminent citizen of Savannah, Georgia. It was David Bushnell, in search of sanctuary. Baldwin never repeated the story his college mate told, whether of shame and disgrace, or the weariness of long years of hope defeated. Bushnell, by his friend's aid, became a schoolmaster in the back country, and sardonically taught children their letters and the rule of three. Then, at the age of nearly sixty, he satisfied the simple requirements for the practice of medicine, and settled in the village of Warrenton, Georgia.

For twenty-five years, good Dr. Bush physicked and bled the country folk. He died in 1824, at the age of eighty-two, leaving a savory memory. Not until his will was published did anyone know that the village doctor hid one of the great inventive geniuses of his time.

He left a considerable property, which was delivered to the children of his deceased brother Ezra, in Saybrook, "together with some curious machinery, partly built, which had been viewed by several gentlemen, none of whom, I believe, have been able to determine what it would have been, if it had been completed."

The emotions of dead men, freed from time, wander about to disturb other minds. I am still troubled by silent old Dr. Bush of Warrenton, keeping a pledge of anger against his own youth, his own ardor.

New York's City Hall, and in the background at the left, Trinity Church, in which Maggie Moncrieff and Captain John Coghlan were united in most unhappy matrimony.

6 Sweet Maggie Moncrieff

Among those mortals most richly endowed by the capricious favor of fortune must be reckoned the celebrated Aaron Burr, no less honored for his aid to the young republic than notorious for the fatal delinquencies of his moral character. Favorably distinguished by the fair sex for the graces of his person, he commended himself to the learned by the precocity and solidity of his attainments. His attendance at the College of New Jersey had been crowned by the diploma of that learned institution, conferred upon him at the early age of sixteen. In the year of our independence he attained, in his twentieth year, the rank of major. And in that year Miss Margaret Moncrieff plighted to him her tender troth.

Major Burr was aide to General Israel Putnam, commanding the army defending New York. It was the month of June, and the pastures of the island were green, the gardens of the townspeople in full flower. The army's headquarters were established in the Warren house, at the corner of Broadway and the Battery, a spacious and elegant mansion accommodating, in addition to the staff, the General's wife and his two daughters. These estimable ladies, with others of their kind, aided in giving to the Revolutionary War something of that respectable, domestic character commonly lacking in the contests of brutal soldieries.

The paternal instincts of the good General Putnam were awakened one day by the receipt of a pathetic missive from a certain Margaret Moncrieff, daughter of Major Moncrieff of the British army. She was held by Revolutionists, in Elizabeth Town; longing, in vain, to join her father, who was with the British troops on Staten Island, she begged the privilege of a safe conduct.

"Dear mam," replied General Putnam, with that orthography which grieved his aide, who had helped to found the Cliosophic Society in his freshman year, "I must beag your pardon for not answoring your leators sooner but the reason was becaus I did not know how to give you an answor, and not becaus Majr. Moncref did not give me my tital for I dont regard that in the least, but am willing to do him or any of his any kind offes lays in my power not with standing our political disputs for I know let his sentements be what they will he must fight and am well assured we shal fight sooner than give up our Libertys. According to your desir I have been trieing to git leave for you to go to Staatons Island. . . .

"Yestorday Majir Leavenston [Livingston] was hear and said you had a mind to com to New York but all the lades of his acquantone was gon out of town and asked my consent for your coming her as Mir'st Putnam and two Daughtors are hear, be assured if you wil com you shal be hartely welcom and I think much more likely to acomplesh the eand you wish for that is to see your father."

General Putnam was not a man to let war interfere with the sacred obligations of friendship. At the Battle of Bunker Hill, having perceived a British friend, Colonel Small, alone and exposed to the fire of the American line, he saved the colonel's life by turning aside muskets and crying, "Kill as many as you can, but spare Small!"

The fair petitioner soon arrived, under the escort of an American colonel. Although but fourteen, she foreshowed that beauty which was later to be famed in the annals of unsanctified love. Her first act was to become enamored of the General's aide, in whom she felt a secret and lawless ebullience responsive to her own. In the point of gallantry, says Burr's first biographer, who knew him well for forty years, "he was excessively vain, and regardless of all those ties which ought to control an honorable mind. In his intercourse with females he was an unprincipled flatterer, ever prepared to take advantage of their weakness, their credulity, or their confidence. She that confided in him was lost."

Pretty Margaret confided, and, in the sober judgment of Burr's biographer, was lost. Her own memoirs, it is true, tell only of an attachment conceived in honor and prosecuted with maidenly decorum. The historian will, however, admit only with reluctance a lady's memoirs as evidence. "O!" she cries, "may these pages one day meet the eye of him who subdued my virgin heart, whom the immutable unerring laws of nature had pointed out for my husband, but whose sacred decree the barbarous customs of society fatally violated. To him I plighted my virgin vow, and I shall never cease to lament that obedience to a *father* left it incomplete. . . . With this *conqueror* of my soul, how happy should I now have been! . . . O, ten thousand times happier should I have been with him, in the wildest desert of our native country, the woods affording us our only shelter, and their fruits our only repast, than under the canopy of costly state, with all the refinements and embellishments of courts, with the royal warrior [the Duke of York] who would fain have proved himself the conqueror of France."

Into this opening bud of love there crept a worm, a serpent into this mutual cup. Aaron Burr, it is said, delighted to watch the deft fingers of lovely Margaret limning the summer flowers

of Broadway's gardens. Studying, however, with amorous intensity such a water color, his heart quaked with a dreadful suspicion; the flower design, destined for her father, followed with
horrid exactness the outlines of the new fortifications of Manhattan Island!

A still more dreadful suspicion is entertained by one of
Burr's biographers: that wanton Burr, having made his conquest, was nonplused what to do with it. He, a Princeton man,
had little appetite for seeking with his beloved some desert, with
the woods for their only shelter, and fruits their only repast. If
the biographer's surmise be just, the story of the treacherous
flower painting is an invention of the faithless deceiver, wearied
of the sight of his victim.

It is true that Margaret herself gives, in her memoirs, some
cause for suspicion. Though she was seldom allowed to be
alone, her chief delight, she confesses, was to escape to the
gallery at the top of the house, and to view with a telescope
the British fleet and army at Staten Island. And in the presence
of the great she displayed an indecent pertness. "One day after
dinner, the congress was the toast; Gen. Washington viewed me
very attentively, and sarcastically said, 'Miss Moncrieff, you
don't drink your wine.' Embarrassed by this reproof, I knew
not how to act; at last, as if by a secret impulse, I addressed
myself to the American commander, and taking the wine I
said, 'General Howe is the toast.'" All were vexed at the girl's
temerity; but General Putnam, whose heart was composed of
those noble materials which equally command respect and admiration, averred that General Washington should not be af-
fronted by such a child. Washington relented; "Well, Miss,
I will overlook your indiscretion, on condition that you drink
my health, or General Putnam's, the first time you dine at Sir
William Howe's table, on the other side of the water."

For one reason or another, it was determined that the disturbing Miss Moncrieff should be removed farther from the

scene of the war. She was sent to Kingsbridge, and placed under the chaperonage of General Mifflin and his lady. When, at length, her return to her father was arranged, she was delivered to Staten Island in the twelve-oared barge of the Continental Congress, with General Knox and his suite for escort. Arriving at the flagship of Admiral Howe (brother of Sir William), and being ushered into the wardroom, she heard the pleasing buzz: "She is a sweet girl; she is divinely handsome!" Asked for a toast, she remembered her promise, and gave General Putnam. A shocked colonel upbraided her, saying: "You must not give him here!" But courtly Admiral Howe interrupted: "O! by all means, if he be the lady's *sweetheart*, I can have no objection to drink his health." After this evidence of warriors' good-fellowship, matching that of their foes, Miss Margaret presented a letter from her American protector:

"Ginrole Putnam's compliments to Major Moncrieffe, has made him a present of a fine daughter, if he don't lick [i. e., like] her he must send her back again, and he will provide her with a good twig husband."

"The substitution of *twig* for *whig* husband," she remembers humorously, "served as a fund of entertainment to the whole company."

Not long after, the British succeeded, by the Battle of Long Island, in forcing the Americans out of Manhattan. Margaret returned, to shed a melancholy tear on the scenes enshrined in her heart by sacred memory.

She was not long permitted to indulge in the rites of amorous fidelity. A British captain, John Coghlan, saw her at an assembly, and without consulting her heart or deigning to ask her permission, demanded her in marriage, and won her father to his purpose. This Coghlan had made the tour of the world with Captain Cook as a midshipman, but had been demoted for drinking, quarreling, and threatening to knife the cook. He was social and convivial, could "set the table in a roar," as the saying was, and was accounted one of the hand-somest men of his time. He was, however, extravagantly devoted to the fair sex, and yielded all too readily to every fashionable vice and folly.

Margaret conjured her suitor to act as a man of humanity; he replied that he valued not her refusal, so long as he had the Major's consent, and with a dreadful oath, he swore that her obstinacy should not avail her. At length, yielding to the anger of her parent, she accepted the importunate lover. But she took, as she confesses, a viper to her bed.

They were married in Trinity Church, on February 28, 1777, by the Rev. Dr. Auchmuty. Hymen showered none of his blessings upon the pair. Captain Coghlan soon sold out of the army, took lodgings in New York, and introduced his fifteen-year-old wife to libertines and women of doubtful character. A year later, the couple returned to England, and a long story of adventure and misadventure began.

The husband took a solitary house in Wales, with the de-sign to break her spirit or her heart. She escaped, and made her way, penniless, to London. "Lovers pressed around me at every inn; Hibernia's gallant sons, some of whom had seen me in Dublin, made the most liberal offers, and uttered the warmest vows," to which she obdurately turned a deaf ear. She took refuge with a friend of her father's, Lord Thomas Clinton, later Lord Lincoln. General Gage, famed in Revolutionary annals, took charge to her, at her father's behest, and placed her in a Dominican convent at Calais. Thither, when she was oppressed by the dismal circumstances of All Saints' Day, when the ladies of the society were assembled at midnight to view the bones and skulls of the dead, taken from Mother Earth and placed in cof-fins in the chapel, came Lord Thomas Clinton. "Youth," as she truly says, "is the season of credulity, and flattery never yet was unwelcome to a female ear." She fled with Lord Thomas from her doleful surroundings.

Henceforth her life was to lie in the half-world of a reprobated society. She learned to cajole her shame with the vain seductions of luxury, and to direct her affections at the bidding of interest. For a time she consecrated all the emotions of friendship to that bright luminary of genius, Charles James Fox. But "the giddiness of extreme youth, and the remarkable levity of my disposition, was not calculated to secure the attachment of this illustrious character." She made the tour of Europe in company with a Mr. Fazakerly, cultivating her understanding and gaining a worldly polish. Nevertheless, "as to real happiness, I never enjoyed it under the auspices of this gentleman." She formed the acquaintance of Lord Hervey, and with him possessed, for several months, all the comforts and delights of domestic life, until he was appointed envoy to a foreign court. She had an unhappy passage with the Duke of York, second son of George III, finding in him little candor and ingenuousness. "Fidelity to vows is not the virtue of Princes. During my hard distresses in a horrid gaol, often did I apply to this Royal Lothario, this perfidious Lovelace—and the fruit of my application was silence! Beware, then, ye of my unhappy sex, how ye are beguiled by the gew-gaw of Royal Splendor!"

Burdened by debts, she found it best to transfer her seat to Paris, in 1788. There, in the last mad days of the Old Régime, she led a life of frantic and expensive gaiety. She was eventually honored with a *lettre de cachet*, signed by the king's own hand, consigning her to a verminous prison for debt. She was later released, on the ground of pregnancy, by the good office of the Comte d'Artois, brother of the king. The kind count deigned to act as her protector. But, having lost her chariot and post-chaise, her clothes and jewels, she ventured back to England, only to fall into more distresses with her creditors and sharping lawyers. She knew the inside of a spunging house, and was confined for two years in King's Bench Prison. There she was delivered of a child, without assistance, for no doctor was admitted after 10 P.M., and "the life of a woman is not considered as worth preservation, at the expense of breaking through the established rules of a gaol." The child remained naked for two days, until an unknown friend sent her two guineas.

Misfortune plagued her by more than natural ways. She dreamed that she saw her father's funeral, with her youngest brother as chief mourner, and on the coffin a bleeding heart. So veritable seemed the vision that she put on public mourning. Some time later, she learned that her father had died on the date of her dream, December 10, 1791, in New York, having burst an artery of the heart. He was interred, so she says, in Trinity Churchyard, his ashes being mixed with those of his old friend Colonel Maitland. The situation of his tomb is no longer to be discovered.

In this dismal latter end of gallantry—she was only twenty-nine years old!—she brought action against her unfeeling husband, who was publicly excommunicated in his own parish church. He came to no good, indeed, at his finish. He died in a public hospital, in 1807, and his body was detained a fortnight in the vain hope that some relation might step forward to pay the last sad duties. Of the end of Margaret Moncrieff I can tell you nothing, but I much fear that it was solitary and obscure.

She wrote her memoirs in 1792 to touch the heart of the British nation, and persuade it to pay her debts, desiring also to bring pain to certain former lovers. She recognized all too well the lesson of her tragic life. She hoped, with the unheeded pathos of those who contemplate the wreck of their youthful dreams, that her example might benefit the giddy fair ones of her sex, tempted to stray from the path of virtue without adequate pecuniary compensation. "Beware!" she cries in a moment of deep feeling, "beware, ye lovely victims of their crocodile caresses! While the sunshine of fortune beams around you, while the bloom of beauty lasts, and the charms of novelty hold their sway, waste not your precious hours in unprofitable idleness and wild extravagance. Make the false dissemblers, while they pay homage to your beauty, provide also for your interest; lay up stores against a *rainy day*."

A French contingent in Revolutionary America, as seen from the British point of view

7 Denis-Jean Dubouchet
in the
American Revolution

It was a strange army that made the American Revolution—overwhelmingly amateur and commanded by farmers, lawyers, physicians, booksellers. With the hayseed generals and the chawbacon colonels mingled the French volunteers.

The French were diverse: some were self-sacrificing idealists, like Lafayette; some were devoted and competent officers, like Pierre Charles L'Enfant, who later made the plan of the city of Washington; some were outright ne'er-do-wells, fleeing their own ill fame at home. The French had little in common except the courage to cross perilous seas and do battle for a noble but desperate cause. Most of them proclaimed their eagerness to die for America's freedom from England, France's ancient enemy; but most of them harbored mixed motives—republican enthusiasm, delight in adventure, and ambition for glory and distinction, at a high rate of combat pay.

One of the French volunteers was Denis-Jean Florimond Langlois Dubouchet, born in 1752 to a family of the minor nobility, an army family that put its sons in the service and married its daughters to officers. He joined up at fourteen, and went to the artillery school at Bapaume to take the entrance examinations for the officers' training course. While waiting for the exams he fought a duel and was wounded, seriously, he says, but not too seriously to flee the threat of official punishment for dueling. (All too many gentleman officers seemed bent on killing friend instead of foe.) He escaped to Luxembourg and joined an Austrian regiment composed mostly of French deserters. He did not like the Austrian service; for one thing, his uniform was so tight that he could scarcely breathe. He succeeded in shifting to the French army; he fought briefly in Corsica and was stationed here and there in France. He was only a lieutenant; promotions, in the stagnant peacetime, were slow. He dreamed vainly of glory, honor, and a rise in rank and pay.

In 1776 America declared its independence and improvised an army. General Washington sent urgent requests to the American commissioners in Paris, headed by Silas Deane, to recruit a few competent engineering and artillery officers. Deane interpreted the request liberally. He engaged some capable specialists, who served the Revolutionary army well; he also made incautious promises and even more incautious hints and intimations to a swarm of slippery swashbucklers and bravos.

Among the first to volunteer was Thomas Conway, an Irish colonel in the French army, who had married Dubouchet's sister. Conway interviewed Silas Deane in Paris, and was assured that he would be at least a major general in America. Dubouchet, thirsting, as he admits, for laurels, honors, pensions, and lands, decided to offer his sword to free the oppressed from their bonds. He was well aware that a major general's brother-in-law is not overlooked in any army.

Conway and Dubouchet took passage in a supply vessel surreptitiously carrying arms to America with the connivance and backing of the French government. The ship swarmed with French officers filled with at least temporary republican zeal. It arrived in Portsmouth, New Hampshire, in mid-April, 1777, after an eighty-eight-day crossing. The French were greeted enthusiastically as liberators by the massed populace.

Colonel Conway left immediately to carry dispatches from Silas Deane in Paris to the Continental Congress in Philadelphia. There he was well received and was commissioned brigadier general. Congress thought its appointment handsome, but Conway did not. He should have been a major general, wrote Dubouchet, "much more properly than M. de La Fayette, a mere cavalry captain in France." Conway's disgruntlement resulted in the alleged "Conway Cabal," which, according to a rather doubtful story, aimed to oust Washington from command of the armies.

Dubouchet and his party journeyed to Boston, where they were politely received by Major General William Heath. Dubouchet found Boston a well-built city, with a fine port. "The people are Puritans, grave, of extreme austerity of behavior; they never laugh. According to their laws a heavy fine is imposed, and even, for repeated offenses, imprisonment, for singing or playing cards or frequenting taverns on Sunday."

Dubouchet and a brother officer, Lieutenant Thomas Mullens, another Irishman in French service, bought horses and set out to join Conway in Philadelphia. "We traversed a superb country, fairly well inhabited, very fertile." The two had a chance to show their spirit in a wayside inn. "It is customary, when people drink together in English America, to propose toasts or healths. Not to reply to them is an insult. We found installed in the dining room a man of middle age, who fell into conversation with Monsieur Mullens. Soon he called for a bowl of punch and proposed that we drink of it. We accepted; nothing appeared likely to trouble the harmony of our gathering, till suddenly Monsieur Mullens' fist landed in the middle of the American's face, covering it with blood. As I did not yet understand English, I could not imagine how such a sudden quarrel had broken out. Monsieur Mullens, violent and irascible by nature, didn't stop there. He kicked the man out of the house; and the innkeeper, to my extreme surprise, seemed to applaud what he was doing. As soon as [Mullens] had regained some composure I asked him what could have driven him to such extremes. He told me that the victim, ill intentioned toward the American government, was talking disrespectfully of General Washington, and had just refused to drink to his health; and that Mullens had undertaken to punish his insolence the more willingly as the scoundrel had just made some impertinent remarks about the French officers recently arrived from Europe. The exit of the victim rectified everything; this action brought Monsieur Mullens the reputation of being a good Whig, a man singularly attached to the cause of independence. The story, to his honor, spread; it was even told to General Washington; and though he disapproved of the violence of the action, he could not help laughing at it."

At another inn the two officers were awakened by a tumult below. They descended to the parlor, to find in progress an informal judicial inquiry on a case of *bondelage*, bundling, that quaint native custom permitting lads and lasses to share a bed, under proper guarantees. "The rules permit innocent caresses, all the affection proper to brother and sister; anything more is rigorously forbidden. In this case the confidences of the girl divulged enterprises of an odious nature. The young man had been unable to confine himself to permissible favors; he would have invaded the conjugal domain, had not the girl's courageous resistance interposed an obstacle. The tribunal of public opinion held that he should be forever barred from the Temple of Hymen. The decree would have been enforced by the agreement of all the maidens concerned with the observation of the laws of bundling had he not obtained his pardon and promised before us all to take the offended girl to wife the following week."

Dubouchet and Mullens reported at army headquarters in Morristown, New Jersey. General Washington gave them an honorable but cool reception, "in accordance with his reserved, thoughtful character." (In accordance also with his irritation at the arrival of a throng of young French adventurers expecting high commissions in the new army, despite their ignorance of English. The clever ones had made a deal with Silas Deane in Paris; thus the Chevalier de Borre forced on Washington his appointment as brigadier general. Dubouchet regretted that he had not had equal foresight; he had been too exclusively concerned with *la gloire*.)

As no commission appeared for Dubouchet, he wrote a letter to Washington (May 20, 1777) pointing to his sacrifices and his ardor, honor, and gentility, and avowing that he learned with pain that the General planned to employ him only when he should learn English. Dubouchet ended by offering to join any regiment of grenadiers as a gentleman volunteer.

On June 3 he received a commission as a mere captain, "out of consideration for Conway." He was deeply offended; was he entitled to no consideration for himself? He was tempted to return the commission, but, hiding his sufferings, he drilled the soldiers of Conway's brigade in French army exercises. Thus he demonstrated that even a swaggering Frenchman could accept discipline. Some of his companions, who had come to America only to escape French justice, had already tarnished the French reputation: "They befouled the name of Frenchman by their profound immorality. I tried daily to destroy these distressing impressions."

He made the acquaintance of the army's eminences. He worshiped General Washington, already world-famous, who dominated the army by his character and spirit. Dubouchet describes his insight, his force of mind, his power of conceiving great plans, his calm courage, his imperturbable self-possession. "He possessed all human perfections." He admired also Colonel Alexander Hamilton, brilliant and competent. "His enlightened mind, his political and military talents, made him very worthy of his post." He knew also Generals Greene and Knox; and Lord Stirling, impressive and well-mannered, though a toper. ("I saw him completely drunk at a party on 24 June 1777.") Rumor said that Stirling was fighting not for liberty but out of resentment because the title of Lord, readily accorded in America, was refused him in England on the pretext that he was the son of a baker.

Dubouchet's report of army and civilian morale is contradictory. At one moment he admits the general indiscipline and discouragement; at another he describes the general patriotic enthusiasm, with recruits signing up and asking no pay. (They were not likely to get much, anyway.) White-haired fathers, he says, would bring in their sons to enlist; fiancées would agree to marriage only when their young men should have made one or two campaigns.

Since Dubouchet did not like his subordinate position, nor in fact the company of his brother-in-law Conway, he decided to join the northern army, which was then retreating south from Ticonderoga before Burgoyne's invasion. He asked permission of General Washington to join General Horatio Gates. This was granted with suspicious readiness.

He set forth, alone and on foot, on August 8, 1777. He paused in Philadelphia, which he describes as clean and well planned, but monotonous in its uniformity. Not only did all the houses look alike, but their inner arrangements and their furniture were disposed according to a common plan. Churches of every sect abounded, for tolerance was a reality, and no bad effects were visible. The Quakers, kindly, industrious, pure in manners, dominated society. The surroundings of the city were charming. Nature was cheery and fecund, and an air of abundance hung over the handsome country houses. "In this fine country is every means of happiness for men who, far from the vices of our old Europe, establish themselves here. The climate is moderate, the soil fertile, the cities picturesque; it is a new

Eden. The women are agreeable of feature, svelte of figure, well-complexioned, amiable of character, and possessed of an iron fidelity. They have all the virtues that make the glory and adornment of their sex."

On his way north he was much indebted to women's hospitality. "Americans cordially offer their produce, bread of a savory whiteness unknown in France, and excellent fruit. They give this not for money, but out of a kindness and simplicity of manners worthy of the Golden Age."

It was nevertheless a painful journey. He found himself spitting blood; he had a regular evening fever. Most of his hair fell out. In Albany he stopped to buy a wig. He could find only one, very large and red; it covered most of his face and almost met his coal-black eyebrows.

Dubouchet found the American army in Stillwater, twenty-four miles north of Albany. General Gates received this haggard, travel-stained grotesque coolly, if not suspiciously. "What do you want?" he said abruptly. "Opportunities to gain your esteem, General. For this I have left Washington's army. Will Your Excellency permit me to join the front-line troops as a volunteer?"

This mild request Gates granted, with the observation that he wished all Frenchmen were as reasonable and moderate in their claims. He went further, inviting Dubouchet to dinner at his mess. At this function, remarks were made about foreigners who thought their rank and office should demand deference and appointment to high place in the American army. The foreigners, it was said, displayed an indecent arrogance. Far from taking offense, Dubouchet agreed with the critics, admitting that many of his compatriots had fled Europe to escape punishment for misconduct. He was applauded for his frankness, and complimented on his English, which was rapidly improving.

General Gates assigned Dubouchet to Colonel Daniel Morgan's famous corps of riflemen or rangers, mostly frontiersmen armed with the deadly Kentucky rifle, longer-ranged and far more accurate than the English musket. Colonel Morgan, "the Old Wagoner," controlled his woodland sharpshooters with a hunter's turkey-call. Dubouchet found in the ranks the Chevalier de Kermorvan, a Breton officer who had served in Turkey as colonel and who held a lieutenant-colonelcy in the American army. The Chevalier had, however, provoked Washington and his staff by his criticisms of operations; the post he coveted, Chief of Engineers, was assigned to Kosciusko, the famous Polish volunteer. Kermorvan seems to have joined Morgan's rangers merely to see some action before returning to France.

Dubouchet went to headquarters to ask for a tent. "They are only for soldiers," said Gates more than brusquely, implying that a French volunteer was no proper soldier. Humiliated, Dubouchet retired. He cut branches with his sword and contrived a little hut, with three boards for roof and three to serve both as floor and bed. He had only his overcoat for blanket. At any rate, he says, he was better off than Robinson Crusoe.

General Burgoyne was now attempting to push his army south to Albany; Gates faced him in the woods and cleared meadows of Bemis Heights, above the Hudson River. After a period of stalling, when both sides waited for reinforcements, the armies came to grips on September 19, 1777. Dubouchet describes this encounter, variously called the First Battle of Bemis Heights, or of Freeman's Farm, or of Saratoga. The British sent out skirmishers (*enfants perdus*), not planning a pitched battle. But the Americans responded so vigorously, sharpshooting from the forest's edge, that the main British army was committed. It was hot and bloody work. "The noise of musketry and artillery was magnified by the echoes resounding in the hollow." By nightfall the battlefield, still in British hands, was heaped with dead and dying. "Both sides claimed victory; both have exaggerated their achievements and the losses of their opponents." At least the Americans proved that in a hand-to-hand encounter they could stand against the well-drilled red-coats and Hessians.

Next day Gates made his inspection of the advanced posts. He summoned Dubouchet, gave him a handshake equivalent to a French embrace, and said: "I recognize by your valor a French gentleman; everyone has spoken of it. You did yesterday numberless courageous deeds, which fill me with great esteem for you." He pointed to Dubouchet's wretched cabin, ordered his adjutant to provide a tent, and invited the Frenchman to dinner.

On October 7 followed the Second Battle of Bemis Heights, which ended British hopes of invasion. In the action Dubouchet took command of a leaderless company, which captured an enemy battery. On a field piled with dead, Gates brevetted him major.

On the seventeenth Burgoyne capitulated. In the sportsmanlike manner of the century, the victorious Gates invited the vanquished generals to dinner in his tent. The banquet table was formed of planks laid across two half-barrels. The two glasses were reserved for the rival generals, while the other guests drank rum and cider out of small basins. Gates, with mockery or gallantry, offered a toast to His Britannic Majesty, and "Gentleman Johnny" Burgoyne replied with a health to General Washington. Burgoyne, sitting opposite Dubouchet, pretended not to see him, thus tactfully seeming to overlook the unofficial French alliance with the rebels. So Dubouchet interprets Burgoyne's disregard; but perhaps Gentleman Johnny could not look calmly on the red wig.

Dubouchet's evening fevers continuing, he decided to return to France. Though he ascribes his resignation from the American army to ill health, he admits that he foresaw war between England and France emerging from the American Revolution, and he wanted professional profit from it. "Service far away for an ill-assured power seemed to me less likely to be rewarded by our government than services under our own flag. I took care not to announce this motive, and merely alleged my weakened health, which demanded a rest of several months for its re-establishment." Lafayette, informed of his decision, wrote him a flattering letter: "I am very sorry that your poor health obliges you to leave us. It is always a pleasure to find oneself in a foreign country with compatriots who behave as you do." Dubouchet offered to carry dispatches from the Congress to Franklin in Paris and to return. "To tell the truth, nothing was less certain than my return to America. . . . I did not dwell much on this final proof of my zeal."

He took leave of Gates, receiving many kind words from the commander and from Benedict Arnold, Benjamin Lincoln, Daniel Morgan, and others. In order to receive his official discharge from the Congress he walked and hitchhiked in bitter December weather to York, Pennsylvania, where that body was sitting. Congress passed a resolution complimenting him and ratifying his promotion to major. President Henry Laurens gave him a packet of dispatches for Franklin. He proceeded (for a military man always proceeds, he never goes) to Annapolis, where he found a French vessel sailing for Haiti. Thence he could make his way to France.

Five days out, the ship met a heavily armed English corsair and was commanded to stop. While the boarding party approached, Dubouchet had time to strip off his uniform and throw it overside, with his dispatches from Congress. But his money and his testimonials from Congress, Lafayette, and others he thrust into his boots. At his request the captain added his name to the ship's manifest as a ship's officer.

The ruse was not successful. The boarding party clambered up the side; the officer in charge said to Dubouchet: "Have you ever seen New York harbor?"

"No."

"Well, we're going to take you there. You'll enjoy it; it's

the finest harbor in the world."

"Sir, decent men do not insult misfortune, they respect it!"

"Put this insolent and disrespectful prisoner in irons, at the bottom of the hold!"

To the bottom of the hold Dubouchet went in irons. But after twenty-four hours without food he was released by the English captain, and received the forced, unwilling apologies of his captor.

In New York he was consigned to the prison ship *Judith*, a floating hell, stinking, swarming with vermin, ridden with dysentery, scurvy, the itch. It was during a winter of unexampled cold, and many had their feet frozen. The five hundred prisoners were released from the "foul cloaca" of the hold at fixed hours, to breathe. "Even the air was measured out to us." The prisoners could hardly hope to survive more than a few months. At the daily distributions of loathsome food, feeble struggles took place. "Woe to him who was too weak to drag himself to the food-issue! He was counted as dead." Dubouchet subsisted for twenty-four hours on a piece of bacon and a little oatmeal flour, which he cooked on a shovel. Many committed suicide. When one desperate man jumped overboard the captain shouted: "Let him alone! He insists on dying; you must not use force on anyone!"

A drunken guard, without provocation, struck Dubouchet on the head with his musket; only his tall hat saved him from a split skull. Two Irish guards, sympathizing with a fellow Catholic, crossed themselves and furtively passed him half a loaf of bread.

But after only three weeks on the *Judith*, fortune came to the Frenchman's aid. Uproar on deck indicated that the guards were more than usually drunk. The noise dwindled; in the dusk, Dubouchet and six others stole on deck, ran to a small boat on the foredeck, cut the lashings, put her overside, and jumped in. The aroused guards fired at them, but missed in the darkness.

The fugitives' situation was desperate. The city, largely Loyalist, was held by the British; friendly country lay far away. They had no proper clothes for midwinter and no food, and their boat was leaky. Nevertheless they rowed out to lower New York Harbor; no doubt the tide was running out. They found there a strange ship at anchor, and took the desperate chance of hailing her. She was in fact a French *parlementaire*, which had come under a flag of truce to parley with the English. This business done, the ship was waiting for a wind to sail for Haiti. The runaways were taken aboard and hidden, for fear of a British search. When indeed a boarding party appeared, it took only a perfunctory look around, for the fugitives' small boat had drifted back to New York on the returning tide and had stranded there; the hunt was centered in the city.

Thus Dubouchet got safely to Haiti. He then came down with fever, and was lodged with a kindly free mulatto woman. She made no indecent demands upon him, he reported, unlike most of her kind, "who assail especially young men newly arrived, not yet enervated by the climate and by excesses."

After a long bout of illness he recovered and returned to France, arriving at the end of July, 1778. In Paris he called on Franklin, and found to his relief that the great man had received duplicates of the dispatches Dubouchet had delivered to the sea. He was warmly received by John Adams and Richard Lee.

Although he felt himself entitled at least to a French colonelcy for his American exploits, he experienced the usual setbacks of the absentee and was forced to settle for a captaincy. Family influences, however, worked to make him an aide-de-camp to Rochambeau, who was then preparing the great expedition in aid of the American Revolutionary armies. Unexpectedly, Dubouchet found himself headed back to the United States.

After a stormy ninety-day crossing, Rochambeau's forces arrived in Newport, Rhode Island, on July 11, 1780, and were joyfully received as liberators. Dubouchet was appointed aide-major-général, and because of his knowledge of English he became, in effect, liaison officer with the Americans, military and civilian. He enjoyed this association and helped to keep good relations with the inhabitants, as they testified with a Resolution of Thanks from the city on his departure.

After a full year in Newport the main French army moved out, in July, 1781, for the campaign that was to end at Yorktown. But Dubouchet was left behind, as chief of staff of the base detachment assigned to Newport. He was angry and humiliated at the slight. A fellow officer, M. de Laubardière, offered to buy his horses, saying that in the circumstances Dubouchet wouldn't need them. Dubouchet took the words as irony or persiflage, and responded bitterly. Laubardière, considering himself insulted, asked satisfaction.

The two, with a certain M. de Mauduit serving as second to both contestants, walked to the outskirts of the city, and at the word of command fell upon each other with their swords. Laubardière received two slight wounds, while his thrust at Dubouchet "would have transfixed me, if his weapon had not been arrested by the collar-bone." M. de Mauduit helped pull out the weapon, and then walked Dubouchet back to his billet, in the house of the worthy Captain Storey at 265 Thames Street. "The great quantity of blood I lost in walking back made my wound the less dangerous," wrote Dubouchet, subscribing to the then-accepted theory of bloodletting. "Aided by a large cloak in which I was wrapped I bore myself so hardily that a number of people, asking me for orders, were surely far from imagining that I was wounded and covered with blood." On reaching Captain Storey's house, Mauduit hurried off to fetch the army surgeon.

Dubouchet entered; the daughter of the house, Miss Betsy, asked him to take tea. "Being very impatient to reach my room, and not to prolong the conversation on the stair, I imprudently promised to do so." In his room he did his best to staunch the flow of blood, and felt himself grow steadily weaker. "The young person, probably finding that I was too slow in keeping my promise, came to summon me, and entered at the moment when, without my cloak and bloody shirt, I was sponging my wound. This sight, so new, so unexpected to her, filled her with such terror that, with a scream, she fell back in a faint. Her screams and the noise of her fall immediately brought her father and mother from the ground floor. They found me trying to bring her back to consciousness by pouring water on her face. . . . But she did not respond, and her parents were ready to despair when my surgeon arrived, happily, to attend to her and to bring her out of her faint with strong cordials." Dubouchet was put to bed and was bled (!) three times in twenty-four hours. Nevertheless he recovered in seventeen days, and made his peace with the convalescent M. de Laubardière.

In August, Dubouchet, with the Newport detachment, was ordered to join Rochambeau in Virginia. He was present at the Battle of Yorktown and at Cornwallis' capitulation on October 19—four years, almost to the day, after Burgoyne's surrender at Saratoga. Unfortunately Dubouchet gives us no piquant details to add to history's store.

In February, 1782, Rochambeau sent Dubouchet with a shipload of English prisoners to be exchanged for American prisoners at New York. As he lay outside the harbor, the British Commissioner of Prisoners came aboard. He kept looking at Dubouchet and saying: "Major, I can't help feeling that I've seen you somewhere." "It's very possible, my dear Colonel," said Dubouchet, "you must have travelled much, and so have I."

Dubouchet brought back 104 released prisoners as exchanges. From them he caught jail fever, or typhus, which put him into a delirium for nineteen days. Convalescent, he paid a visit to General Gates, who had retired to his pretty farmhouse by the Potomac, near Shepardstown, West Virginia.

He then embarked with Rochambeau for the expedition to the Caribbean, returning to France in 1783.

Dubouchet was rewarded for his services in America by advancement in the French army, by letters and testimonials of leaders from Washington down, by a silver medal from Franklin commemorating the recognition by France of American independence. "Franklin said that as I had so distinguished myself and as I was the only Frenchman who had fought both at Saratoga and at Yorktown, I had every right to it."

But Dubouchet was not satisfied. At the war's end the Americans formed the Society of the Cincinnati, composed of American officers. It admitted likewise French officers who had worn the American uniform for three years, and generals and colonels in Rochambeau's army. Dubouchet was clearly ineligible. Nevertheless, he hungered for the Society's medal, which depended from a sky-blue ribbon and bore on one side a bald eagle and Cincinnatus importuned by the Roman senators to leave his plow, and on the other side Cincinnatus returning to his family. Dubouchet had never desired anything so much. After being turned down by Lafayette and Rochambeau, he decided to plead his case in America.

Thus, at the end of March, 1784, he embarked at Lorient on a fast packet. He landed in New York, paused hardly a moment, and hurried to Philadelphia, where the Society was meeting under Washington's presidency. General Knox presented Dubouchet's application for membership. It was unanimously accepted, and Washington signed the appointment with kind remarks of approbation. Dubouchet immediately returned to New York and caught the return trip of the French packet. He was in France again after an absence of only three months. Surely few have gone so far, so long, so uncomfortably and dangerously, for a medal. But the conquest of the boutonnière brought him more joy, he says, than did that of the Golden Fleece to Jason.

Back in France, Dubouchet resumed his army career. Like most officers, he remained at his post after the outbreak of the French Revolution in 1789. But when Louis XVI was arrested in 1791 every French soldier was forced to question where his allegiance lay. Dubouchet was denounced by a renegade priest as a reactionary. He resigned his commission and, with a false passport, escaped to Worms, where he joined the émigré army of the Prince de Condé. This army was mostly occupied with balls, parties, and disputes about social precedence. After a year of inactivity, Dubouchet ventured into France to rescue his wife and son, whom he had left in Paris. He was caught; his false *certificat de résidence* had been delivered to him by a double spy, who was actually an agent of the revolutionary government. Imprisoned in Grenoble, he became, deliberately, a gay comedian, president of the jolly *club des incarcérés*. He found, as have others, that nothing disarms grim inquisitors so much as amusing lightheadedness. Having established his harmlessness, he was transferred, after nine months, to a makeshift prison, a former seminary. From this he escaped in mid-December, 1793, and made his way to Switzerland. The account of his adventures would make a fine addition to the literature of escapes and perilous journeys.

He lived, penniless, in Lausanne. He communicated his needs to a friend in Lyons by writing a comic song full of double meanings. This a lady friend, bound for France, cut up and wore as curl-papers. But the efficient revolutionary police knew the curl-paper trick; they stripped the lady's head and interpreted the message. The friend to whom it was addressed was ruined. Dubouchet's wife died of hardship in Paris; his sister's mother-in-law, Mme Conway, mother of Washington's general, eventually escaped to Switzerland, bringing Dubouchet's son.

Now began a long period of wandering in central Europe, in Würtemberg, Prussia, Poland, Bohemia, Austria. Dubouchet lived by many expedients, especially by teaching English. He endured all the sufferings of the émigrés, everywhere unwelcome.

After the amnesty of 1802, Dubouchet and his son returned to France, but found there no means of livelihood. Napoleon became Emperor in 1804; Dubouchet persuaded himself that his duty was to serve the new imperial France in his soldier's trade. A commission as brigadier general was the decisive argument. As he was now nearing sixty, he served as the sedentary commander of forts at Ypres and Breda. But when the Allied army advanced against Napoleon in 1814 he rediscovered his legitimist convictions and prudently resigned his commission. He did well. After Waterloo he was rewarded by Louis XVIII with the title of Marquis and the rank of lieutenant general, which comported a comfortable pension and no duties.

Some time after 1822, in his seventies, he wrote, with elderly satisfaction, the memories of his career. (The manuscript, unpublished, reposes in the Cornell University Library.) Looking backward to his youthful experiences in America, he reflected that he had been misled by his callow enthusiasm for liberty, a word full of maleficent magic. The American Revolution was sedition, a rebellion against legitimate authority; it should have been stifled at its outset. The French participation in the American Revolution was a calamitous error of policy. Most of the young French gentlemen of the court who went to America became ardent proselytes of a new order in France; they were the first to profess and propagate antisocial doctrines, subversive of all rules; they armed themselves against authority, undermined the throne, brought revolution and disaster to France, to Europe, to the world.

Thus does the old self reprove the young self. But its lessons, like the lessons of history, always come too late.

General Aquila Giles, by Gilbert Stuart

8 Aquila Giles;
Lover on Parole

Major Aquila Giles of the Maryland Continentals was taken prisoner at Germantown early in 1778. He was sent to the village of Flatbush, in our Brooklyn, billeted with a sulky Dutch family, and put on his parole not to escape. With a hundred other American officers, he shared the ennui of the dismal village, which the paroled gentleman chose to call Limbobush or Limboshire.

Food was scarce, with a British army in Manhattan and an American blockade ringing the city. The prisoners of war breakfasted on warm water faintly flavored with tea, on stale butter, and on bread half-baked, for fuel was dearer than food. They dined on clippers (clams) and supped on supon (mush), sometimes with skimmed milk, more generally with buttermilk blended with molasses, a mixture kept for weeks in a churn, fermenting to the Dutch taste.

Boredom filled their days. They could, indeed, climb to the Heights of Brooklyn to watch in vain for a French fleet. Or, if a little wine or spirits fell into their hands, they could organize a horrid banquet with whisky and clippers, madeira and mush. At one such festival, it is recorded that Major Giles sang "How Stands the Glass?" and "Although the Taste of Battle." He gave for his toasts "The United States of America" and "Miss Betsy Shipton."

His companions drank piously to the first toast, slyly to the second. They knew the way of things, for a stricken heart can find no hiding place amid the intimacies of prisoners. They knew Miss Betsy, or more properly, Miss Eliza Shipton, the niece and ward of Colonel William Axtell, a rich and powerful Tory.

Colonel Axtell's ardent loyalism was that of the recent convert. He had preached rebellion until the British, sweeping over his land to win the Battle of Long Island, won his devotion. As a prize for his change of faith, he received the commission of colonel in the British forces, with orders to raise a regiment. He drew full pay, clothing, arms, and provisions for a corps of five hundred men. He was attended by his aide-de-camp, chaplain, physician, surgeon, and secretary. The colonel obtained, however, only about thirty recruits. These were encamped on his grounds and employed in guarding his house, poultry, hogs, sheep, and cows. They were known officially as the Nassau Blues, but in Flatbush as the Nasty Blues. They termed themselves the Holy Ghosters.

Colonel Axtell received the lucrative duty of licensing all the public houses of the county and also the right of issuing passes to cross on the ferry to New York. He immediately raised the passage rate from twopence to two shillings. The envious calculated that, as some twenty thousand people passed the ferry annually, the privilege brought Colonel Axtell £2,000 a year.

Colonel Axtell, a man who could recognize and embrace opportunity, was clearly destined for prosperity. He had a fine house in Flatbush, the most elegant in the village, containing even a ballroom and a secret chamber, in which the colonel was several times forced to take refuge. The house stood at the junction of the present Flatbush and Parkside avenues, a region now a continuous crag of apartment houses built upon a substructure of delicatessen stores.

Colonel Axtell, the formidable uncle, requiring deference from all the village, could not command the heart of his niece. The ladies, arch baggages, take all masterfulness as a challenge; rebels, they cleave to rebels, in despite of policy. Eliza Shipton found it piquant to coquet with the dashing Maryland major across her picket fence, the first in Flatbush. The major discovered in her conversation a charm against prisoner's ennui. Soon each perceived in the other inestimable qualities of spirit, sweet harmonies of taste, common jests, mutual objects of scorn. They were in love.

They corresponded with the aid of obliging go-betweens. Their letters, still preserved by the New-York Historical Society, may be consulted by the serious student. They are charming letters, telling the story of love that had its way over the wars of nations.

The major rallied Eliza on her subservience to her uncle. With tongue in cheek, he quoted from one of "Gentleman Johnny" Burgoyne's dramas:

> Duty in female breasts shou'd give the law,
> And make ev'n love obedient to Papa.

He was submissive and adoring, and once at least, at some sort of party, he was foolish. He let slip a sally to the tune that ladies have no sentiment of honor. His apologies are pitiful to read. He would fain have begged the pardon of all the ladies present. "Far from thinking that the Ladies do not possess sentiments of honor, I am of opinion that they retain the most refin'd. Cou'd I induce myself to believe otherwise, I shou'd not continue to hold the sex in that esteem I have ever done. You can witness how great my affection has been for *one*."

Courtship came to its destined end, the hand of Eliza was

asked and surrendered, and the vows were exchanged. But the case was a hard one. The heiress of the rich and haughty colonel to wed a rebel prisoner! They dared make no avowal to the grim uncle. And the lips of Flatbush were pursed, the heads of Flatbush ominously shaken.

The lovers suffered more than their share of lovers' pains. Eliza, in a gush of heroic self-denial, bade Aquila forget her forever. He replied that such an act was totally out of his power. He protested: "Oh my dear, my darling Eliza, the thought of your suffering mind distracts, torments me, makes me miserable. I cannot, will not, allow so noble, so generous & so amiable a woman to languish, & I the cause. Yes, my dearest girl, a very short time shall put it in your power to change the situation, I hope, agreeable to your wish."

Eliza spoke her love in the language of the hoop skirt and whalebone period. Stiff and stilted it may appear, but it tells the same story as the limp prose of this uncorseted era. And bosoms bound by stays heaved, it would seem, very prettily: "I wish with all my Heart, my G [She called him "my G, "no doubt because she could not call a romantic lover "Aquila"], I wish with all my Heart, my G, your Eliza could send you an invitation to her lovely quarters. Nancy and the Col. just gone. I really feel melancholy, nothing to interrupt my cogitations except now and then the foot of my little faithfull Ranger gently laid on my Arm, as if acquainted with the feelings of his Mistress' Heart, and wished to tell her he would go and fetch the lovely youth who possesses so large a part of it; indeed I *believe* I may say the whole; of this I am *sure*, that I have lost it, and I know no bosom so likely for it to of taken refuge in as yours. Search— and if you find yourself really in possession of the poor little Fugitive use it tenderly, hide it, oh hide it from the rancorous Eye of Envy, nor expose it to the maligant snear of Malice, remember, remember, it is a sacred deposit, and you must be responsible for its safety. I intended to of made my appearance in your part of the World this morning, but Boreas, that unfeeling Deity, terrified me with the threat of metamorphosing me into a statue of Ice about mid way, and there leaving me as a monument to all presumptuous lovers who dare defy his powers; probably by tomorrow morning his rigors may abate, if not, as '*Amor vincit omnia*' I will brave his fury with a smile—happy we, if seated in some soft clime where gentle Zephyrus reigns, our walks uninterrupted by any northern blasts, but all the sweets of Natur wafted to us (delighting our senses) by each faning breeze—what do you think of the Poets of Arcadia? methinks I should like to become a shepherdess of that happy region with you the dear shepherd and companion of my Hours.

> In the same field our flocks we'd feed,
> To the same stream our Heifers lead,
> Nor would I, if I could be free,
> But boast my loss of Liberty."

Aquila could tune the oaten pipe as well as Eliza. He sang his love in Arcadian strains:

> I yield, I yield, resistless fair,
> Oh spare the heart you've won,
> And kindly listen to my prayer
> Or Eliza I'm undone.

The news of their romance, a delicious tid-bit for Flatbush, was soon conveyed beyond the bounds of that village. The Tory ladies of New York were inclined to look with a kindly eye on this proof that love was still mightier than policy, that Venus still vanquished Mars. A Mrs. Sutherland drove to Flatbush one day. Alighting at the Axtell house, she exclaimed:

"Pray, Miss Shipton, who is that genteel, handsome young Man setting there?"

"That, Ma'am, is Major Giles."

"Is it indeed?" Mrs. Sutherland smiled archly. "It is a great pity, my dear girl, he is not on our side of the question."

"Indeed, I am quite of your opinion. If that were the case I would not answer for the consequences."

"No; neither will I answer for the consequences, as it is."

"Why, I hope you do not suspect my loyalty?"

"Indeed I do not; but—"

"But, what?"

"Rebellion is not to last forever."

"True; but I am a little of the opinion it will outlast my youth."

Eliza gleefully reported the conversation to her genteel, handsome G.

Inevitably, some blabber brought the news of Eliza's pranks to her uncle's ear. He flew into a proper rage and put his heavy foot down. Eliza was imprisoned in the house. She found her only solace in secret correspondence with her G. She dared even to write under her uncle's nose. "You will think I have a vast deal of temerity when I tell you that I am writeing at the same Table with my Uncle. . . . The old Gentleman begins to look as if he had an inclination to know who I am scribbling to, so I think I had best fold up as fast as I can."

The old gentleman had recourse to the ancient remedy for the ancient ill. He would distract his niece's mind. He would carry her off to gay Manhattan for the winter (1779-80), that she might find surcease in its brilliant routs and in more eligible suits a new master for her heart. Aquila, helpless in Flatbush solitudes, was inconsolable. "I hope that when the cruel hour of separation comes she will think of me, and aliviate my situation, by constancy and her literary productions." Unworthily, he hinted that her heart did not share the agony of his own. "Ah cruel, too cruel fortune, how long am I to continue the object of your displeasure—oh change the scene, & let some person that's yet a stranger to your *whims* take a share. . . . I've one consolation, however—you will have some relief from your cruel, unjust and ungenerous imprisonment, indeed that's a very great consolation. I wish you every pleasure and happiness whilst among the *gay* and the *great*."

Eliza seems indeed to have found distraction in New York's society. She gives us testimony to the Loyalists' round of pleasure, while Washington and his men froze and starved at Morristown. She writes: "No, I cannot come Monday, 'tis impossible, so many engagements to prevent me. This evening to a little Hop at Mrs. Sutherland's, tho' I don't think I shall hop much, for I never was so much fatigued after a dance in my life as I am this morning. Tomorrow I am engaged on a visiting expedition, I wish it was over as it is a formidable affair. Sunday to dine at Minto [the home of her friend Miss Jauncey], Monday to go to the play with Gen'l Phillips, who always enquires after you, under the appellation of my Pett. . . . On Tuesday we have a party to Tea on board the Fanny, and on *Wednesday* I shall visit your blest retreat."

Amid the intoxicating gaieties of New York her heart remained true. Her friend Sally Browne wrote to Major Giles: "I know you are impatient, the sweet creature is very well and echoes every sigh you waft across that cruel river." And Eliza added by way of postscript:

> The Hills, the Dales, the groves remain,
> But Damon there I seek in vain.

Her New York friends found in her constancy a proof of sensibility and of Cupid's might. Her rebel Pett was the subject of jest, but of no scorn.

In the spring of 1780 Eliza and her lover both suffered from ills of the body as from those of the heart. They exchanged sympathy and counsels. Eliza describes her "long, lank, meagre appearence, with sunk Eyes, hollow Cheeks, pale Lips, and Bones with all imaginable impudence stareing every one that comes near me in the face. I wish they would grow a little more modest and get themselves cover'd." Eliza, the first to recover, took the rose as her ensign; the major, she mocked, preserved the color of the leaf. He adopted the pretty conceit and addressed one of his letters merely: "From the Leaf to the Rose."

Eliza passed the summer of 1780 in Flatbush and found means of seeing her lover. Their dalliance at length became unendurable, to themselves as to the suspicious uncle. Eliza wrote, on September 20: "I dare say when once I am removed from him I love best in the world I shall be better treated."

We have not Aquila's answer. No doubt he contrived a meeting and summoned Eliza to the bold, the romantic solution of their woes. Eliza escaped her prison; the two were married before mid-October.

Loyalist society looked fondly on the mettlesome pair. Gallant General Phillips promised a parole to leave the British lines for Eliza and her Pett. No doubt many were glad to score off the greedy Colonel Axtell, profiteering faster than a gentleman should.

Even that tyrant uncle was brought round. The French army had landed in Newport, and the war seemed to linger on forever; the triumph of the British arms was no longer a sure gamble. Colonel Axtell accepted the rebel major into his family with the best grace possible, considering him as a form of property insurance against the rebel success. It was even whispered, though certainly falsely, that Colonel Axtell had secretly arranged the prudent match.

After Yorktown, the uncle, now the sage and well-beloved uncle, made over his property to his niece. He retired to England at the evacuation and lived tolerably on his colonel's half-pay, awarded him for his meritorious service in defending his own livestock.

Aquila and Eliza occupied the Flatbush mansion after the Revolution. It is not clear if Aquila bought the confiscated house for his bride or if he was able to enforce her claims to ownership. For a number of years he led the life of a gentleman farmer, holding as well the office of marshal. He was one of the founders of Erasmus Hall, that famous school, and was a patron of music. He became brigadier general of militia. During the War of 1812 he was a major general. He retired on a pension in 1818.

Aquila and Eliza had several sons, one of them a scapegrace who was dismissed from West Point for insulting an officer. The parents' thoughts dwelt upon duty and obligation, and upon material concerns. They ceased to quote from the poets. They were happy, no doubt, but their placidity does not touch us. That is always the curious thing about history; out of the universal death only old emotion, old passion, really exists, living in our response to passion.

Count Axel Fersen

9 Axel Fersen
in America

No queen has received more posthumous affection than Marie Antoinette. A steady throb of emotion, discernible on two continents, can be traced to her adorers. As the symbol of all aristocratic virtue cut down by the ravening mob, she gathered to herself, through a long century, the attributes of saintliness.

But today the historians assure us of her frailty. Professor Alma Söderhjelm of the University of Åbo, ferreting in the old papers in a Swedish country house, has discovered the best evidence that Marie Antoinette had a lover, Count Axel Fersen. (There are even some who assert that Fersen was the father of Louis XVII, the unhappy Dauphin of the Temple. They can present no proof—only enough suspicious circumstances to embarrass a whole College of Heralds.)

Though the queen has lost her good name, this naughty generation loves her only the more dearly. Here is evidently a lesson for our times.

Count Axel Fersen was a great lover, who risked death several times in vain efforts to save his royal mistress from the guillotine. He organized her escape from the Tuileries, which brought her within a few miles of the royalist troops and freedom. During her later captivity, he spent two days concealed in her quarters. After her execution he never smiled again, but spent his life in vain efforts to league Europe for vengeance. Nightly he recorded his grief in his diary. He met his death at the hands of a Stockholm mob, on an anniversary of the flight from the Tuileries.

Axel Fersen was of the stuff of the romantic hero, the gallant knight. There is a tradition that still lingers in Newport, Rhode Island, that he also wooed Miss Eliza Hunter of 264 Thames Street, across the street from Miss Betsy Storey, who figured in the adventures of Captain Dubouchet.

It was on the eleventh of July, 1780, that Rochambeau and his army arrived in the harbor of Newport. The city was hardly more than a modern village in size, but it was one of our chief seaports, rich with the profits of the slave trade. The official welcome was bright and noisy. Thirteen grand rockets were fired in front of the State House; every burgher was issued thirteen candles to burn in his window. "The Quakers did not chuse their Lights shd shine before men, & their Windows were broken," wrote President Ezra Stiles of Yale in his diary.

The outward rejoicings hid some private forebodings. The citizens considered their new allies, says a French army chaplain, "mere idolaters, in short, a kind of light, nimble machines, deformed to the last degree, incapable of anything solid or consistent; entirely taken up with the dressing of their hair, and painting their faces; without delicacy or fidelity, and paying no respect even to the most sacred obligation." It was, therefore, with alarmed cordiality that the householders received the officers billeted upon them: rakish young gallants, with cued hair, plumed, cockaded hats, white uniforms, heavily epauletted, frogged with gold braid, faced with the regimental colors.

The Duc de Lauzun, one of the leading menaces to the virtue of the French court, found himself lodged with Mrs.

Deborah Hunter. Only thirty-six, and the mother of four, she had already lost her husband, Dr. William Hunter, a famous anatomist and the first patron of Gilbert Stuart. Mrs. Hunter's father was Godfrey Malbone, of the Newport Malbones. Her oldest daughter, Eliza, was just eighteen. In her presence the Duc de Lauzun, who kept a valuable record of his amorous triumphs, exhibited a novel restraint. "I never fell in love with mesdemoiselles Hunter," he notes with an air of surprise. "But if they had been my sisters, I could not have been fonder of them, especially the eldest, one of the most charming persons I have ever met." He was equally devoted to the mother, who treated him as a son, and who took "the most touching care" of him when he was ill.

Perhaps Lauzun contained his emotions out of respect for his bosom friend, Count Axel Fersen, aide-de-camp to General Rochambeau. Fersen, although billeted elsewhere, was constantly at the Hunters'. He was the handsomest man in the French army, according to Newport reckoning. (Indeed, years later the poet Herder cited him as the handsomest man he had ever seen.) His blue eyes, heavily browed, had a calm and slightly melancholy look; his mouth, with very mobile lips, was small, his nose straight and finely chiseled, his nostrils small and delicate. He was tall and blond; "big Axel," the king of Sweden called him affectionately. His manners were simple, but with the poise of ancient nobility. The Duc de Lévis says that he was circumspect with men and reserved with women, serious without being melancholy. "His face and manner would exactly suit the hero of a novel; but not a French novel; he did not possess the brilliancy and lightness for that rôle."

Fersen became a fixed ornament of the Hunter drawing-room. He ventures, even in letters to his father, one of the leading statesmen and one of the proudest nobles of Sweden, to mention the charming Eliza Hunter, "pretty, sweet, gay, and a very good musician. I go there every evening, but without its being serious." Fersen adds, in letters to his sister, details which would have caused the father to knit his noble brow. He stays at the Hunters' every evening till midnight, after Lauzun has retired. Eliza plays the piano and sings; he plays his flute. He is teaching her French; she is teaching him English. Already she speaks French charmingly. "These evenings are very agreeable."

Eliza Hunter was, indeed, of a sort to rouse concern in a haughty father. A Mr. Chipman of Boston wrote in his journal: "We had heard much of Miss Hunter, of Rhode Island, who was at Dr. Lloyd's; we were prepared to expect something supernatural. We called to see her; our expectations were exceeded by the interview. She is, without exception, the most beautiful, accomplished, and elegant person (with a mind, if possible, as we were informed by her friends, superior) that I ever beheld." A miniature in the possession of her grandniece, Miss Anna Falconnet Hunter of Newport, shows a winsome and wistful face, demure, still guarding its secrets. Through one of the little whims of fate, a member of the Hunter family later married a relative of the Fersens. And Miss Hunter had ever a tiny portrait of Axel Fersen, the gift of his kin, above her Newport hearth, beside Eliza.

In those long winter evenings, Axel told Eliza of his boyhood in the ancestral castles of Ljung and Mälsåker, and of the gay court of Gustav III. He had played the part of an English jockey in a French comedy before the nobility assembled at Gripsholm. With his sister Sophie, he had danced in a ballet, a pastoral of ribboned shepherds. King Gustav, a romantic monarch, had organized a medieval tourney, lasting three days; and Axel, in armor, had fought with lance and sword, while the ladies of the court paraded anachronistically as Greek goddesses in gilded chariots.

Perhaps, too, in moments of indiscretion, he told Eliza how he had been distinguished by the loveliest and maddest queen of Europe; how Marie Antoinette, at a masked ball, had made up to him, to the dismay of the courtiers; how she had bidden him to her quarters to show her his Swedish uniform, in which she professed an extreme interest. And of that summer afternoon by the Trianon when he had taught the queen of France to sing with him the old Swedish folk song *"Skära, skära hafre! Hvem skall hafren binda?"* ("Reap, reap the oats! And who, then, shall bind 'em? That my dearest lover will! And where shall I find him?") And of another afternoon when, during a summer shower, he had lingered so long in a private shelter with Her Majesty that he had caught many a sly and questioning look. And how, at length, tongues had begun to wag, and he had prudently chosen to join Rochambeau for a long exile from France.

Midnight confidences and tender reminiscences did their usual work. If the story is true which Eliza's nephew told to his daughter, and which his daughter told to me, Axel Fersen asked Eliza Hunter to marry him. Barely a woman, a commoner, a provincial of a small American town, she was the rival, and the successful rival, of the queen of France.

Her triumph was brief and secret. The family story goes that she refused Axel's hand. Her eyes, she said, were troubling her greatly. The doctors, doing their clumsy utmost to give her comfort, had told her mother that to the best of their knowledge, and barring some miraculous operation by a great London surgeon, she was doomed to lose her sight.

Whether in fact she refused Fersen for this reason, or whether Fersen prudently hesitated this side of a proposal, we do not know. We might have known had not Fersen's intimate diary from 1780 to 1791, charged with compromising secrets, been burned by a friend during the French Revolution.

At least, Fersen sang her praises to a companion. A year after the army had left Newport for its great campaign, the Prince de Broglie visited the town to verify the inflamed reports of Newport beauties he had had from the French officers. "We hastened to pay the due tribute of admiration and gallantry to the Misses Hunter. The elder, without being regularly pretty, has what might be called a noble ensemble, marked by social grace. Her face is finely cut and intelligent; she is graceful in all her movements; she dresses at least as well as Miss Champlin, but is not absolutely so blooming, *whatever Fersen may say*. Her sister, Nancy Hunter, is perhaps less noble, but she is a rose in human form; her character is gay, her face forever laughing, and her teeth charming, which is very rare in America."

(The deplorable teeth of Americans frequently struck the French officers. One of them observes that many handsome American girls of eighteen or twenty are entirely without this precious ornament. He ascribes their case to the excessive consumption of tea and warm bread.)

The girls of Newport made, indeed, the happiest impression on the young Frenchmen, familiar though they were with the belles of Versailles. "Nature has endowed the ladies of Rhode Island with the handsomest, finest features one can imagine; their complexion is clear and white; their hands and feet usually small." Especially noteworthy was the liberty accorded them, and their utter lack of interest in married men. At a series of balls the friendships were cemented; and, says a contemporary letter, the "decent gayety and hilarity which characterized the assembly afforded a convincing proof of the general satisfaction the alliance caused to both nations." The purity of manners on which all eyewitnesses insist suggests that the army had received some remarkably telling lectures from its commanders.

In June, 1781, the French army was at length ordered to the front to join in a vigorous campaign against the British in New York. Every house in Newport was the scene of leavetakings. Axel said farewell to Eliza, I know not how.

The march from Newport to Westchester, in the yellow-green of the American June, delighted the expeditionaries. Indeed, whoever has marched with an army must feel with them the excitement of topping the little stony hills of Connecticut, the pleasures of the deep woods, the humors of the campfires, the alert sense of danger, the sweet fatigue. Everywhere the natives turned out to see the brilliant show, which contrasted sadly with the sight of our own ragged Continentals. The uniforms were white, white and green, black and red; the artillery wore blue with red facings, white leggings and red pompons, short Roman swords at their sides and firelocks in slings. The fine brass fieldpieces were richly ornamented with wreaths and other decorations, and were engraved with baptismal names and boasting mottoes. When the army encamped at a village, the military bands, of which the Americans were extravagantly fond, would give a concert. "At such times officers, soldiers, Americans of both sexes, all intermingle and dance together; it is the feast of equality."

The army made its way, by Plainfield, Willimantic, Hartford, Waterbury, Danbury, and Bedford, to its camp, on the hills west of Hartsdale. It lay west of Central Avenue and south of Harts Corners Road. The archeologist of the future will have a pretty time distinguishing its entrenchments from the bunkers of the Sunningdale Country Club, which overspreads its site.

Fersen saw the indeterminate skirmishing around New York. On August 19, he was sent to Newport with dispatches, riding two hundred and twenty miles in thirty-six hours. After only a day's rest he returned to Westchester, to find the army marching north to Peekskill.

He served honorably throughout the campaign. He left an important record of the operations at Yorktown, and was honored with the Order of Cincinnatus. He passed a dreary winter at Williamsburg, Virginia, the town of which we are so proud, and which he termed a "miserable little hole." Confirming his reputation as a furious horseman, he made a round trip to Philadelphia, seven hundred miles, in seven and a half days.

When, in 1782, the French army made its return journey to Boston, Fersen took leave to revisit Newport "to see my friends and say goodbye to them." In December he set sail to his greater destiny.

It is possible that he once more saw Eliza. As her eyesight steadily grew worse, her mother took her to England in 1785 to consult the best of oculists. And in 1790 or 1791 Fersen was in London, making a desperate effort to enlist aid for the king and queen of France from their brother monarchs. (The Prince of Wales remarked him at an assembly, recognized him as Marie Antoinette's favorite, walked twice round him, looking him up and down; then, announcing "He is certainly a handsome fellow," walked off without an introduction.)

Eliza never returned to London. She lived in England, then in France, settling in Pau with an English companion. The science of the doctors was helpless; she was most of her life practically blind, consoling herself only with music. She died in 1849, at the age of eighty-seven. Axel Fersen had been dead thirty-nine years.

Deborah Sampson

10 Private
Deborah Sampson,
U.S.A.

Not all the heroes of our Revolutionary War fought solely to remove from our shores the tyrant's heel. There was, for example, Miss Deborah Sampson, who found service in the Continental Army a welcome change from teaching school.

Miss Sampson was born in Plympton, Massachusetts, on December 17, 1760. She came of most eminent Puritan stock; among her ancestors were John Alden, Miles Standish, and William Bradford. But the Puritan virtues, in some of their vessels, were already turning a trifle rancid. Her father, after unlucky speculations, could not bear the spectacle of his family's destitution, the sound of their reproaches. He went quietly away.

Deborah, from the age of ten, was put to service with a farmer of Middleboro. She had some opportunity for schooling, which she assiduously improved. When she was released from her indentures, at the age of eighteen, she was able to teach in the infant school of the village.

Some ferment, improper for schoolmistresses, was working in her virginal veins. She longed to travel, to see the world, to perceive with her own eyes the glories of New Bedford, Providence, Boston even. Adventure was her desire, and freedom—the freedom permitted to young men, and denied to a tender female.

She conceived an audacious project. With her own hands she spun and wove cloth, and employed a tailor to make it up as a suit for a gentleman. In this disguise she went to a nearby village and enlisted in the Continental Army under the name of Timothy Thayer. She signed the muster roll and, with her bounty money in pocket, repaired to a tavern, called for spirituous liquors, and behaved in a noisy and indecent manner. She crept finally to her lodging, hid all evidence of the frolic, and resumed her post in the infant school. In the succeeding days, her new feminine elegance was remarked upon. The authorities, searching for Timothy Thayer, were eventually led by village suspicions to her door. She confessed, and was obliged to refund the unspent portion of the bounty money, but was not otherwise punished.

Now, certainly, she found herself in an awkward pass among the townfolk. The village's spiteful references to the bounty money, and the prayers of the brethren who came to labor with her, determined her to be gone. She donned her male costume and set out to see the world, with the smallest of baggage. The minutes of the Middleboro First Baptist Church, for September 3, 1782, report: "For some time before [her departure, she] behaved very loose and unchristian like, and at last left our parts in a sudden manner. . . . It appeared that as several brethren had labour'd with her before she went away, without obtaining satisfaction, concluded it is the Church's duty to withdraw fellowship."

"The Earth," muses her friend and biographer, Herman Mann, "which is computed to be 25,038 English miles in circumference, and to contain about 199,512,595 square miles of surface, is indeed a large body." This did our heroine discover, ere she had contemplated many of those square miles. She

visited Taunton, Rochester, and New Bedford. The captain
of a cruiser offered to take her to sea as his waiter, but she re-
fused, learning that his good-fellowship on shore was changed
to austerity at sea. She turned north again, trudging as far as
Bellingham, halfway between Providence and Worcester.
Here, being destitute, she again enlisted in the Continental
Army, using the first and second names of her brother, Robert
Shurtleff Sampson.

This second enlistment is dated May 20, 1782. The Battle
of Yorktown, in the previous October, had practically ended
the war. In March, Lord North's war ministry was succeeded
by a cabinet pledged to peace. During the negotiations, the
armies rested on their arms, the British in New York, the Americans and French in the Highlands. New recruits at this period
could foresee little likelihood of a hero's death.

Private Deborah was issued a handsome uniform: a blue
coat lined with white, with white wings on the shoulders and
cords on the arms and pockets; a white waistcoat, and breeches
with black straps about the knees; half boots, a black velvet
stock, and a cap with a variegated cockade on one side, a plume
tipped with red on the other, and a white sash about the crown.
One may wonder that a government-issue uniform, designed
for the classic contours of the male, should readily fit the feminine baroque. But the female of those days was used to enduring
severe pressures; it was merely a question of altering the point
of incidence of the stress. As her penetrating biographer points
out: "It is not improbable that the severe pressure of this bandage
served to compress the bosom, while the waist had every natural
convenience for augmentation." Indeed, it appears that Deborah
had natural advantages for her masquerade. "Her aspect is rather
masculine and serene than effeminate and sillily jocose. Her
waist might displease a coquette, but her limbs are regularly proportioned. Ladies of taste consider them handsome, when in the
masculine garb. Her movement is erect, quick, and strong, ges-

tures naturally mild, animating and graceful; speech deliberate, with firm articulation. Her voice is not disagreeable for a female."

She marched with her company to the Hudson, and was stationed at West Point or in one of the nearby camps. In all the hurly-burly of a soldier's life she preserved the secret of her sex. Most threatening to her security were the compulsory swimming parties. Let me have recourse to the ogling niceness of Herman Mann: "General orders were, every warm season for the soldiers to go into the water, as well to exercise themselves in the art of swimming as to clean their bodies. These injunctions were so strictly in point, that her compliance with them would unavoidably have been unbosoming the delicate secret . . . So, after lying awake the first night, she concluded to be the first to rise at roll call. Accordingly, the regiment paraded and marched to the river. She was expert in undressing with the rest. After they were mostly in the water, what should ravish her ear but the sound of a sweet fountain, that percolated over a high rock near the river's brink. It was thickly enclosed with the aspen and alder. Thither she unnoticed retired. And whilst the Hudson swelled with the multitude of masculine bodies, a beautiful rivulet answered every purpose of bathing a more delicate form. Nor were there any old, letcherous, sanctified Elders to peep through the rustling leaves to be inflamed with her charms."

She was ever obliged to circumspection. "It was noted by the soldiers that she never wrestled, nor suffered anyone to twine his arms about her shoulders, as was their custom when walking."

The chief danger to her masquerade was the prying habit of the medical department. She might never answer sick call; she was obliged to lie ingeniously to avoid vaccination. But she came within an ace of discovery when she received a bullet in her thigh, in bloody Westchester, the Neutral Ground.

There was plenty of action still in that unhappy country, a no man's land thirty miles wide. The British in New York, to supply their troops and civilian population with food, had commissioned several corps of Rangers—Tory refugees, commonly called "Cow-boys." Most notorious was Colonel James Delancey's Westchester Refugee Battalion, which would issue by night from its headquarters in Morrisania to raid the Whig farmers north to the Croton River. In emulation of the Cow-boys, the country bandits with revolutionary sympathies organized in bands of "Skinners," so called from their practice of removing the external layer of wealthy farmers. The ruinous competition of Cow-boys and Skinners ended in a kind of coalition, or merger. The Cow-boys turned over tips on Tory property to the Skinners, in exchange for good Whig prospects. Out of regard for public opinion, they would sometimes skirmish ferociously in view of a village, afterward meeting in the woods to divide the takings.

Occasionally the complaints of the despoiled moved the American Army to a raid. Such raids were popular with the soldiers, who were likely to return loaded with plunder. It was in such a punitive expedition that Deborah received her wound. A mounted party, of which she was a member, was sent from the Highlands along the Post Road toward New York to hunt for Colonel Delancey. They fell in with him beside the Tappan Zee, between Tarrytown and Sing Sing. In the affray she received a sword cut on the head, and, worse, "she found her boot on her right leg filled with blood; and in her thigh, just below her groin, she found the incision of a ball, whence it issued.—Females! this effusion was from the veins of your tender sex, in quest of that Liberty you now so serenely possess."

She was carried by her comrades to the French camp at Crompond, near Peekskill. (There is a discrepancy here; the French had long since departed.) Her biographer would have us believe that she was able, secretly, to extract the bullet from her thigh with a penknife and a needle, and to conceal the wound from the lascivious French. But in a report to the Committee on Revolutionary Pensions many years after, it was alleged that the musket ball was never removed. However that be, it is certain that her sex was not discovered, else she would hardly have been permitted to remain in the Army.

In June, 1783, she was sent with a detachment of troops to Philadelphia to put down a mutiny of soldiers demanding their pay. Here she was seized by a malignant epidemic fever. Carried to the hospital, she was examined by the eminent Dr. Barnabas Binney. "Putting his hand in her bosom to feel her pulse, he was surprised to find an inner waistcoat lightly compressing her breasts. Ripping it in haste, he was still more shocked, not only on finding life, but the breasts and other tokens of a female." He concealed his discovery from all but the matron, and with her connivance had the interesting soldier removed and privately nursed back to health. At her departure, he gave her, evidently, some words of caution. "A remembrance of the Doctor's queries and injunctions was but recognizing the necessity of a garland of fig leaves to screen a pearl, that could glitter without disguise." He entrusted her with a letter to her commander, General Paterson, then at West Point.

The letter contained the news of his discovery. The good general, amazed at the information, summoned Private Deborah, and "thus gracefully addressed her: 'Since you have continued in my service, always vigilant, vivacious, faithful, and, in many respects, distinguished yourself from your fellows, I would only ask—Does that martial attire, which now glitters on your body, conceal a female's form?' The close of the sentence drew tears in his eyes, and she fainted."

The general, apprehensive, perhaps, of further emotional eruptions, procured Deborah's honorable discharge. It is dated October 23, 1783.

Still in male clothing, she returned to Massachusetts and spent the winter doing farm work in the village of Sharon. Here she met an industrious farmer, Benjamin Gannett, who stirred a soft emotion within her candid bosom. "Spring having once more wasted its fragrance from the South, our heroine leaped from the masculine to the feminine sphere. Throwing off her martial attire, she once more hid her form with the dishabille of Flora, recommenced her former occupation."

She was joined in wedlock to the industrious farmer on April 7, 1784.

Gossips of the countryside, who had known her as a rakish soldier and as a jolly farm boy, whispered behind their hands. Her biographer found a triumphant rejoinder to their insinuations. "It is hearsay, that Mrs. Gannett refuses to her husband the rites of the marriage bed. She must, then, condescend to smile upon him in the silent alcove, or grass plat; as she has a child, that has scarcely left its cradle."

War's alarums over, the good soldier dreams of heroisms past and of bonuses to come. Mrs. Gannett petitioned the Massachusetts Legislature, in January, 1792, for Army pay long overdue. The Legislature granted her plea, and directed the payment to her of £34, with a flattering resolution: "Whereas it further appears that the said Deborah exhibited an extraordinary instance of female heroism by discharging the duties of a faithful, gallant soldier, and at the same time preserving the virtue & chastity of her sex unsuspected and unblemished, & was discharged from the service with a fair & honorable character. . . ."

In 1805, she was granted, as an invalid soldier, a Federal pension of four dollars a month. This was increased in 1816 to six dollars and forty cents a month, and in 1819 to eight dollars a month.

She died in 1827. Her husband, surviving, seems to have missed his wife's pension. Several winters of brooding led him

to the conviction that he was unfairly used. If a veteran's destitute widow could enjoy his pension, then why not a veteran's
destitute widower? As his neighbors could find no flaw in his
logic, he sent to Congress a petition, stating his grievances. A
committee considered it maturely, and at length returned a
favorable report, stating that the annals of the Revolution
furnished no similar example of female heroism, fidelity, and
courage. By a Special Act of Congress, in 1838, the sum of
$466.66 in back pensions was awarded the petitioner, who,
while Congress deliberated, had died.

There is one curious thing about the documents in Deborah's dossier. In the petition and certificate of 1792, Deborah
gives her date of enlistment as May 20, 1782. In the later appeals
to Congress, it is alleged that she enlisted in April, 1781, that she
went through the Virginia campaign and the Battle of Yorktown, and was present at the surrender of Cornwallis. The same
story is told by her adoring friend, Herman Mann, whose
ecstatic volume appeared in 1797. He gives a detailed account
of Deborah's adventures through the campaign of 1781. (In
the hot work at Yorktown, her coat was half cut away; a
comrade clapped her on the shoulder, saying: "Friend, fear not;
you are only disfigured behind!")

The discrepancy in dates may be variously explained. Perhaps Deborah, reading her own biography, was convinced
that the printing must be true, and her own enlistment records
at fault. But the cynical will say that Deborah, many of whose
actions betray a certain contempt for conventional behavior,
added a year's service to her record for the benefit of her
biographer. When the book appeared, it became a kind of proof
of her exploits. It could be admitted in evidence with her appeal
for a pension.

She has been hailed, even, as the Heroine of the Revolution. Her female descendants are eligible for membership in
the D. A. R.

The Reverend Mason L. Weems

11 Parson Weems: Virtue's Recruiting Sergeant

One of the most persistent folk tales of American history is that of the boy who could not tell a lie. The first recorded appearance of the story was in Parson Weems's *Life of Washington* (1800). It was told him by an excellent lady, a distant relative of George Washington, who had spent much time in his household.

"The following anecdote is . . . too valuable to be lost, and too true to be doubted. . . .

" 'When George,' " said she, 'was about six years old, he was made the wealthy master of a *hatchet!* of which, like most little boys, he was immoderately fond; and was constantly going about chopping every thing that came in his way. One day, in the garden, where he often amused himself hacking his mother's pea-sticks, he unluckily tried the edge of his hatchet on the body of a beautiful young English cherry tree, which he barked so terribly, that I don't believe the tree ever got the better of it. The next morning the old gentleman, finding out what had befallen the tree, which, by the by, was a great favourite, came into the house; and with much warmth asked for the mischievous author, declaring at the same time, that he would not have taken five guineas for his tree. Nobody could tell him anything about it. Presently George and his hatchet made their appearance. "George," said his father, "do you know who killed that beautiful little cherry tree yonder in the garden?" This was a *tough question;* and George staggered under it for a moment; but quickly recovered himself: and looking at his father, with the sweet face of youth brightened with the inexpressible charm of all-conquering truth, he bravely cried out, "I can't tell a lie, Pa; you know I can't tell a lie. I did cut it with my hatchet." "Run to my arms, you dearest boy," cried his father in transports, "run to my arms; glad am I, George, that you killed my tree; for you have paid me for it a thousand fold. Such an act of heroism in my son is more worth than a thousand trees, though blossomed with silver, and their fruits of purest gold." ' "

The story is greeted today, in cultured circles, only with cries of "Faugh!" and "Tush!" All the elite would wager that little George Washington, when taxed with the offense, vowed to his father that he knew nothing of the matter, or even that he had seen black Cudjo barking the tree with his hatchet. Surely he lied like any normally conditioned child. Surely it was Parson Weems who lied for the greater glory of truth-telling.

But after all, Parson Weems had excellent means of knowing the truth. He lived only a few miles from Mount Vernon, and knew the Washington family well. He was occasional incumbent of Pohick Church, of which Washington had been for years a vestryman. His wife's sister was the wife of Washington's personal physician. There is evidence that the cherry tree story was current before Parson Weems told it. He gave the country tale its perduring form; like Plutarch and Shakespeare, he supplied appropriate dialogue for the historical anecdote. The telling seemed to his contemporaries reasonable, consonant with their own moralizing piety. If now we reject it, it is because we want to make a child George Washington who suits our own ideas of what is admirable. But this is the substitution of our own myth-making for that of the past.

Present-day biographers of Washington regard Parson Weems as they would a silverfish in the bathtub. Valiant debunkers of the Washington legend abuse him roundly for making of that genial, cursing, fox-hunting squire a marble statue of virtue. They pardon the first biographer nothing, least of all his success. Weems's life of Washington sold, through forty editions, hundreds of thousands of copies, and it is still in print. It gave to generations of Americans a model of heroic character. Abraham Lincoln loved it. His borrowed copy, kept in a chink of his log cabin, was spoiled by a sudden rain; he had to work three days pulling fodder for its owner, to pay for it.

After the bold debunkers the shy rebunkers come. After a dozen biographies of Washington that mention Weems only with fury or with loathing, one may examine, with a little tenderness, the Parson and his work.

I think you will find his book charming. True, he is something of a *simpliste* in his interpretation of history's profounder trends and forces. But with what gusto, what vigor, he gives us the human side of the past!

"The news [of the French aggressions along our western frontier] was brought to Britain's king just as he had dispatched his pudding; and he sat, right royally amusing himself with a slice of Gloucester and a nip of ale. From the lips of the king down fell the luckless cheese, alas! not grac'd to comfort the stomach of the Lord's anointed; while, crowned with snowy foam, the nut-brown ale stood untasted beside his plate. Suddenly, as he heard the news, the monarch darkened in his place: and answering darkness shrouded all his court. In silence he rolled his eyes of fire on the floor, and twirled his *terrible thumbs!* his pages shrunk from his presence; for who could stand before the king of thundering ships, when wrath, in gleams of lightning, flashed from his '*dark red eyes*'? Starting at length, as from a trance, he swallowed his ale: then clenching his fist, he gave the table a tremendous knock, and cursed the wooden-shoed nation by his God!"

And this idyllic picture of the Father of Our Country, when at last, his public labors o'er, he could retire to his rich plantation: "How delicious must it have been . . . to have seen his numerous flocks and herds, gamboling around him through excess of joy, and fullness of fat; to have beheld his steps washed with butter, and his rivers floated with rivers of milk; to have seen his once naked fields and frog-croaking swamps, now, by clearance or manure, converted into meadows, standing thick with heavy crops of timothy and sweet scented clover; while his farm-yards were piled with such quantities of litter and manure as afforded a constantly increasing fertility to his lands."

Abraham Lincoln was right. Weems's life of Washington is well worth three days' labor pulling fodder.

Mason Locke Weems was born at Marshes Seat, Herring Bay, Anne Arundel County, Maryland, in 1760. He was the youngest of David Weems's nineteen children. After studying medicine in Edinburgh, he abandoned the scalpel for the Book, and was trained for the ministry in England. He found himself ready for ordination in 1784; but he could persuade no one to perform the laying on of hands. The Revolution had severed the American Episcopal Church from its parent Church of England. The American Episcopalians, episcopalian only in purpose, had not a single bishop; the English prelates refused the benefits of the apostolic succession to the American rebels. As only a bishop can make priests, the American Church was doomed, by a kind of sterilization.

Weems and a fellow-candidate named Edward Gantt appealed to Benjamin Franklin, minister to France. Franklin answered characteristically: "An hundred years hence, when People are more enlightened, it will be wondered at, that Men in America, qualified by their Learning and Piety to pray for and instruct their Neighbors, should not be permitted to do it till they had made a Voyage of six thousand Miles out and home, to ask leave of a cross old Gentleman at Canterbury."

Weems, finding Franklin more amusing than helpful, wrote to John Adams, minister at The Hague, asking if no Dutch, Swedish, or German bishop would undertake to ordain him in the Church of England without an oath of allegiance. Adams discovered the king of Denmark to be eager to aid American souls. The Danish monarch even offered to install a bishop in the Danish West Indies for the convenience of American postulants. In the face of this threat, the English episcopacy relented. Weems and Gantt were ordained by the Archbishop of Canterbury, the cross old gentleman himself, on September 12, 1784. They were the first priests ordained within the American Episcopal Church.

Weems served for eight or nine years, with zeal and industry, in small country parishes of Anne Arundel County, Maryland. In his preaching he practiced the appeal to the emotions. A fellow-cleric, with a touch of professional jaundice, describes his pulpit style: "A certain pitch of voice or rather vociferation with but now and then a distinguishable word of correspondent horror raised the storm probably rather by sympathy than by rational concern."

The rewards, material and spiritual, were small in the country churches and chapels of ease, as they were prettily called in Maryland. Weems's ebullient spirit was chafed. In his irksome leisures he undertook the printing and vending of godly books. He soon discovered that his hortatory eloquence could be bound to service as the handmaiden of salesmanship. About 1794 he entered the employ of Mathew Carey, the Philadelphia publisher, and began a life-long career as traveling book agent.

In the following year he married Fanny, daughter of Colonel Jesse Ewell of Belle Air, Dumfries, Virginia. He removed to that town, near Quantico; then the thriving county seat, it is today a ghost of old glories. As the years passed, his twelve children and the swarm of his wife's relatives obliged him to heroic labors and kept him in permanent debt.

His wife was a superior woman. Weems wrote to his employer: "Mrs. Weems, who is very much my Sovereign in money matters, is unwilling to agree to [your proposal]. The Ladies, you know, are said to be the weaker Vessels, and we must not have such collisions with them as will break the precious porcelain of Peace & Domestic happiness." Her only faults were fecundity and an "impolitic tho' most amiable generosity to her many & lazy country Relatives."

One of the first and greatest of American book salesmen, Parson Weems spent nearly thirty years on the road for Mathew Carey. New York he found an unrewarding territory. "I have been soliciting Purchasers of the Bible the whole day long, and have not been able to find *one*!!! The town is deluged with Bibles and Deism." He was more fortunate in the South, which he covered in his two-horse wagon, loaded with books. He attended court sessions, race meetings, and revivals, for it is well known that high emotions lower sales resistance. Mounted on his cart tail in the town squares, he out-shouted the medicine barkers, or, as guest preacher in village churches, he spoke home to sinners, and knocked at the door of their hearts, with a rousing sales talk for peroration. Bishop Meade of Virginia, hearing him preach within his own diocese, was much displeased because the Parson praised from the pulpit Tom Paine's *Age of Reason*, of which he was carrying an ample stock. The Bishop remonstrated; Parson Weems protested that he sold the antidote with the bane, and offered him the Bishop of Llandaff's refutation of Tom Paine. The Parson's sermons, though much relished, sometimes gave scandal by causing the faithful to laugh out loud. Once, in Fredericksburg, he preached from the text: "We are fearfully and wonderfully made." He concluded abruptly, saying: "I must stop; for should I go on, some of the young ladies present would not sleep *a wink* tonight."

Nor was he loath to pursue customers from the church to the taverns, drinking dens, pop shops and grog pips. To push the sales of his own *Drunkard's Looking Glass* he would enter a dram shop, pretending to be boozy and cup stricken. Having gained the favorable attention of all the drinkers, he would produce his pamphlets, and seldom fail of excellent returns.

His employer, to be sure, did not approve of undignified sales technique. He wrote to Weems, objecting to the posting of advertisements for the Bible in taverns. Weems invoked the highest precedent: "If our blessed Savior . . . had been so fastidious as to leave the poor Beer house, grog pip Gentry to themselves what w^d have become of those miserable grog blossom^d & Carbuncled Devils?"

He was always gay, always one for a frolic. He was a superior performer on the fiddle, which he carried with him to charm his customers and the spirits of his horses and his own on the long roads. Once, after preaching an edifying sermon, he rested at an inn with some strolling puppet-showmen. The showmen's music having fallen ill, he volunteered to be the orchestra, stipulating only that he must sit behind a screen, for the dignity of the cloth. But his renditions being much applauded, he could not refrain from raising his beaming face, framed in long white hair, above the screen to take a bow. This scandal to holy orders is sourly reported by the Bishop of Virginia.

But Weems had a sense of values, a sense of proportion. His high jinks were ever subordinate to his great purpose, salesmanship. He loved his work and he loved books, especially his best-selling Bible, "smooth, fair & spotless as a young Bride."

He confessed to Carey: "I wish you to remember that the Family bible is my favorite book and that I hope to die selling it."

His trials were many; not the least was the abundance of rival laborers in the vineyard. Nor were his relations with his employer easy. His soaring spirit was held in leash by the grim business mind of Mathew Carey, forever looking in his ledgers to dissipate Weems's golden visions. Although each party threatened almost daily to terminate the connection forever, the two continued in an emotional business relationship until Weems's death. Their correspondence, of an unparalleled virulence, consists half of commercial records, half of personal abuse. Weems's command of invective may be inferred from the examples already given of his style; Carey, also a prolific author, could likewise dip his pen in gall. Attempting to compose a political difference, he wrote in this wise to the celebrated Cobbett, the author of *Rural Rides:* "Wretch as you are, I desire not the honor or credit of being abused or vilified by you. . . . I will never disgrace my paper with your detested name. Callous and case-hardened, you draw subsistence from your infamy and notoriety. 'Hissed and hooted by the pointing crowd,' you care not, provided you can amass money enough to secure you a competence at the close of your dishonorable career. . . . Heavens! what pride! what pleasure! I should feel in dragging you reeking from your den, and cow-skinning you till Argus himself should not be able to perceive a hair's breadth upon your carcass but sore upon sore!" The dispute with Cobbett was amicably settled.

The Parson employed his few respites from bookselling in the service of literature. The success of his *Washington* inspired him to write lives of Penn, Franklin, and General Marion, still readable and still read. He applied himself also to the castigation of contemporary vices, in vigorous pamphlets, at a shilling each. Thus he offered a stock in trade for both the quality and mass markets. His pamphlets, "season'd, so Judges say, to the palate of young persons & of the Multitude," often carried the rest of his list. He wrote to Carey, in 1812, the war year: "I assure you my prospects for this year are squally, and unless I can make something by other people's Gambling & Drink, I shall be strongly tempted myself."

His *Hymen's Recruiting-Sergeant; or, the New Matrimonial Tat-Too for Old Bachelors* is an attempt "to wash out the leprous stains of old Bachelorism, and extinguish, if possible, the pestilence of celibacy." He details the eight blisses of matrimony, with racy pictures of the alternatives to which bachelors are impelled. The text is enlivened with excellent songs. Our modern poetasters may well admire the virtuosity of his poem to his own wife, Fanny:

> While some for pleasure pawn their health,
>   'Twixt Lais and the Bagni-O,
> I'll save myself and without stealth
>   Kiss and caress my Fanny-O.
>
> She bids more fair t'engage a Jove
>   Then Leda did or Danae-O.
> Were I to paint the queen of love
>   None else should sit but Fanny-O. . . .

The success of *Hymen's Recruiting-Sergeant* led him to compose "THE DRUNKARD'S LOOKING-GLASS, REFLECTING A FAITHFUL LIKENESS OF THE DRUNKARD, IN SUNDRY VERY INTERESTING REPRESENTATIONS OF THE MANY STRANGE CAPERS WHICH HE CUTS AT DIFFERENT STAGES OF HIS DISEASE; as first, When he has only 'A DROP IN HIS EYE,' Second, WHEN HE IS 'HALF SHAVED,' Third, when he is getting 'A little on the Staggers or so,' And fourth and fifth, and so on, TILL HE IS 'QUITE CAPSIZED,' or 'Snug under the Table with the Dogs,' AND Can 'Stick to the FLOOR without holding on.'"

The pamphlet contained a number of horrid illustrations of drunkards. "Good Judges pronounce them well done for fright'ning." The aid of lyricism was also invoked, as, in fact, it is forever in the war upon rum:

> His face, alas! has lost its red!
> His cheeks their burning hue,
> Ragged and warty is his nose,
> But ah! that nose how blue!

The text consists chiefly of dread examples of drunkards' ends. There is the story of Peter and John Hay, lying besotted on the floor of a burning barn. "Owing to the rarefying effects of the violent heat, their stomachs, being filled with rum and fixed air, were seen suddenly to rise to an enormous size, then burst with a noise as loud as a musket."

The author dwells particularly on the dangers of lying down for an hour's refreshing coma in the gutter. Young America was apparently alive with hunted criminals who would stuff their counterfeit money in your pocket, or would leave in your hand the halter of a stolen horse or even a gore-dripping blade. Juries invariably credited this circumstantial evidence against the protestations of the awakened drunkard, and sent him, too late remorseful, to the gallows.

In other pamphlets, Weems flayed the sins of the gamblers (among whom we are surprised to find Marie Antoinette, brought to the guillotine by her taste for play), the duellists, the adulterers, and the murderers of wives and husbands. They are filled with excellent anecdotes, well done for frightening. Let me cite only the story (from *The Maid's and Bachelor's Friend*) of the gentleman "who took a strong mind to suicide, but lacked the resolution to hang himself." Being apparently bent on hanging, in preference to other means of self-destruction, he bethought him of putting the obligation on the state. He therefore charged and primed his gun, exclaimed:

> I'll tread a track but seldom trod
> And stay no longer here, by G-d!

and rushed to a tavern and shot a billiard player.

The sales of the exemplary pamphlets were great, but the author's ambitions greater. He wrote to Carey: "With y^r resources, you cou'd have [the advertisements] out in 10 days, lathering away among the Gamblers, Drunkards, Adulterers & Sinners at a most heroic rate." He loved his trade, and labored at it mightily. Yet somehow, with all his commissions and his royalties, he never contrived to make more than a bare living.

He died in harness, on the road. In 1825 he succumbed to the fatigues of bookselling in Beaufort, South Carolina. His remains were removed to the family grounds in Dumfries, Virginia.

I should like, some day, to visit his resting place, to pay a little tribute to his gay and virtuous spirit. I should like to put a little inscription on his grave. I was thinking of:

> With moral tales and Bible sales
> He gain^d an earthly glory-O,
> And now he greets in SALEM'S streets
> His finest territory-O.

Creek Indians, with whose tribe the French general Milfort spent a good many year

12 The Astounding Adventures of General Milfort

In March, 1814, the Allied troops, flooding over the French frontiers, were converging on Paris. They met with few impediments; one of the few was the indomitable Brigadier General Milfort, former Tastanegy, or War Chief of the Creek Indians.

The general was living in ignominious retirement in the village of Chestres, near Vouziers, in the Ardennes. After the news of Leipzig, of the crumbling of Napoleon's empire, he fortified his home according to the principles of frontier warfare. Of his vestibule he made a redoubt, whence he could command, through five doors, his court and the ground-floor rooms of his house.

As he reported in an official communication to the prefect of the Ardennes, two hundred fifty Cossacks entered Chestres shouting "*Vive Napoléon!*" to beguile the simple villagers. Representing themselves as French, they interviewed the *maire* and the *adjoint*, and asked to be quartered in a large courtyard for the night. *Maire* and *adjoint*, evidently deaf to Slav accent and blind to uniform, fondly took them at their word and assigned them to Milfort's court. ("I do not doubt that they had

Frenchmen among them," he admits.)

The troops picketed their horses in Milfort's garden, and bivouacked in his court. And at ten in the evening, after a profound silence, they suddenly attacked, with hellish din, the five doors opening on his redoubt.

Milfort occupied his little fort. He was very happy. One man against two hundred fifty, but what a man! A Tastanegy amid the palefaces!

He must tell his own story; any words of mine would diminish his own. "I suddenly hear a loud laugh in my kitchen; there were about a dozen men there opening a trench with axes. I was very pleased, since that was the strongest place of my retreat and my fortress. I run up a little staircase, and I see that the breach was being opened wide enough to pass a man, since they had cut several pieces of wood out of the embrasure of my door.

"I take my watch; I see that Death has just struck 10.15. The first man to present himself before the scythe of Death was a youth of about twenty, with a very delicate and handsome face. I say to myself: 'Unhappy youth, in two minutes thou wilt be in the realms of Pluto!' So saying, I pierce his heart. He utters a woeful cry. The others who were below were laughing loudly, thinking that fear was making him fall. Immediately a big sapper mounts to the assault, and I laugh, murmuring as I pierce his heart: 'A *pourboire* for thee, *monsieur le bûcheron!*' He falls, uttering a woeful cry. And now they laugh no more. They put out the light they had, throw their two dead men out the window, and themselves jump out hastily.

"Those who were in the court had lit a great fire. I then spring to a hoophole I had prepared in advance, which dominated and commanded all my courtyard. My arms were ready and in good condition. I take a double-barrelled gun loaded with six buckshot per charge. Before I set my gun in the loophole, I glance out, and I see a mass of more than two hundred men.

Then I put my gun to the loophole; I take aim at four officers talking together. A French voice speaks: 'Shoot, if you're brave enough!' I let the officers go, and I give him the preference, lodging six buckshot in his belly. He falls, his face in the fire. Then I let the four other officers have the other charge; three of them are wounded. Then I take a gun loaded with slugs, and as they are only ten paces away, I let them have it point-blank. I give them the other barrel, and let the bullets fly among them. I take another weapon and spray them with lead. Then I notice that five men are going to enter my kitchen to turn my position. I take a pistol and drop the leader; the others rejoin the mob. I send three more shots into the crowd. My weapons are now all discharged; I profit by a moment of tumult, and seize my cartridges; two minutes suffice to recharge everything. I begin the dance again, and they start to run. It was like a flock of sheep; I continue to give them policing shots. Suddenly, one of them takes a burning brand, and runs to enter my stable, where I had much wood. I have only one shot left; I make him a present of it. I send the man to the devil, and the brand remains in the courtyard.

"I recharge my weapons. Hardly have I finished when I catch sight of one of the scoundrels, torch in hand. He passes before my door and goes back to set fire to a barn full of wood, grain, hay, and straw. Eleven o'clock had just struck. The fire in my court was extinguished; the men and horses were still in the road along my garden; they were loading the dead and dying in a covered wagon. I notice then a lantern and two men. 'Twas one of my neighbors who was charitably carrying the lantern. The officer was carrying a double-barrelled gun. He sends me a bullet. I, no ingrate, return him another, which immediately sends Charon's bark to call for him. Meanwhile, the fire was making progress in the barn. Two hardy lads wish to enjoy their misdeeds, riding their horses through my court toward the barn. Their crime was well exposed by the great fire which lit up the court. I take advantage of it and kill the pair of them. They are carried off. As the men leave my courtyard with their dead, I send three shots to the bearers. One of them says on leaving: '*Sacré nom de Dieu!*' No doubt he was another Frenchman."

He certainly sounds French.

The enemy retired, leaving General Milfort victor in the unequal battle. The burned barn was his only loss.

He made to his superiors the report from which I quote. If they were puzzled by it, they were too occupied with the fall of an empire to seek its elucidation. It was exhumed and published not long since by Commandant André Lasseray in his invaluable *Les Français sous les treize étoiles* (Paris, 1935). Commandant Lasseray is inclined to accept, in the absence of contradictors, the outlines of the general's story. But he would make one qualification. The effervescent general was always one to leap to conclusions. The chances are that the soldiers whom he sent in such numbers to Pluto's realm were in fact Frenchmen, his own compatriots, allies, friends.

One of the few secure facts in the life of General Milfort is that of his birth, which took place on February 2, 1752, in Thin-le-Moutier, near Mézières. He was christened Jean-Antoine Le Clerc; Milfort is a name he chose, in manhood, for reasons of his own. He entered the Gardes lorraines in 1764, the Lorraine-infanterie in 1766, and there remained until the end of 1774. Commandant Lasseray, who had these facts from his dossier, does not tell us his rank.

Thenceforward his biographer must make a hard choice. He may listen open-mouthed to the general's own reminiscences, as published in his *Mémoire ou coup d'oeil rapide sur mes différens voyages et mon séjour dans la nation Crëck* (Paris, 1802), or he may piece together a record from the sparse indications of several officialdoms.

Let us first hear his own story.

In January, 1775, he took ship for Norway. In Bergen he found a vessel sailing for America. He embarked upon her, for all his purpose was to travel, he did not care particularly where. He came to shore at New London, in the Tucuman.

In the Tucuman? In the Tucuman. But isn't Tucuman on the slopes of the Andes, right in the middle of Argentina? So it is. Milfort inserted under errata: "Not in the Tucuman, in the Connecticut." We all make mistakes.

He visited Boston, New York, Philadelphia, Baltimore, and Yorktown. He seems not to have noticed any difficulties between the colonies and England; he comments only on the antipathy of "Wigth" and "Toris," and of Northerner and Southerner.

He pushed on south and west; he passed through Savannah, Augusta, Orangeburg, and Tugalo. He visited the settlements in the Holston region of eastern Tennessee, a country where most of the men are one-eyed. They are called Crackers, or Gougers, because of their favorite form of drunken sport. Milfort's vivid and horrible account of an eye-gouging contest supplements the well-known descriptions of Chastellux, Elkanah Watson, and others.

Pleasanter to the squeamish reader is his record of a formal dinner among the settlers. His hostess, having heard that in good company one takes tea, sent her husband to sell his tobacco for a half-bushel of the herb. She put the tea in a kettle with a large ham, and boiled it well. She then threw away the liquid, and served the ham on one dish, the tea leaves on another. The party chewed valiantly and in vain on the tea leaves, till the hostess, in a fury, threw her plate at her husband and accused him of bringing back cheap tea instead of good, and spending his money on whisky. The ham, says Milfort, was excellent.

His picture of the ignorance, brutality, drunkenness, and sloth of the pioneers bears the mark of authenticity. It is a good corrective to some of our sentimental regard for their virtues.

These despicable Americans despised the Indians and warned Milfort of their savagery toward the whites. But such was Milfort's repugnance to the Americans that he became curious to see their enemies. He set out from Tugalo southwestward into the bush, across the present state of Georgia. A month later, starving, he was rescued by a party of Creeks, to whom the magic word *français* served as a passport and safeguard. He was brought to the village of Coweta, just south of the present Columbus. Fed and refreshed, he was presented to the great chief, the Beloved Man of the Creeks, the celebrated Alexander MacGillivray.

This remarkable person, called the Talleyrand of Alabama, was the son of a Scotch trader and a Creek mother. He had a good education in Charleston and Savannah; he wrote correct, sensitive, and vigorous English. Casting his life among the Creeks, he became their diplomatic leader and organized them against the encroachments of the white settlers. His method, the classic one of weak states, victim states, was to play the strong neighbors one against the other, the United States against Britain against Spain. He dreamed, even, of a vast confederation of the red men against the white.

MacGillivray, says Milfort, was glad to associate again with a man of education. Milfort was grateful to MacGillivray for many kindnesses and gained in him the staunchest of friends. He soon found the savage way of life preferable to that of civilized Americans. He remained with the Creeks for twenty years.

For two of these years he was wholly occupied with the hunt and with war. "The long and frequent journeys I made, and the color of this nation, prevented me from having any feminine attachments." But once, at a three-day festival, he watched with interest the lascivious Dance of the Serpent, which permits the women unusual freedom. "The women had very easily perceived my lack of eagerness concerning them, and I had some reason to believe that they had formed the project of finding the cause of such coldness. They had me teased by one of the prettiest girls of the town, young, and with an interesting face. The other women had contributed to get her a fine calico skirt, a fine chemise, silver pins, an enormous number of ribbons of all colors fixed to her hair, and five pairs of ear-rings attached in order of size. It was in this *grande toilette* that she approached me and chose me for her cavalier. She seemed to me pretty, compared to the others, and I was easily touched by the special attentions she paid me. After having spent some time at the festival, we agreed to meet in a more secret place as soon as the dances were over. . . ." Milfort followed her to her mother's cabin. The girl ran up a ladder to a grain loft, with Milfort close behind. He plunged into the loft.

"I felt myself seized by four persons, which surprised me very much in a place where I thought to be alone. I saw four women, who made me very gay reproaches on my sobriety. They told me that they had not yet seen a capon warrior (such is the translation of the expression they used), and that I should not escape them without their being assured of the contrary. Although I had just finished dinner, and although my senses were a little excited by the good cheer and by the teasing of the girl, yet the assault seemed to me a hard one to endure. Still, I had to prove to these women that a French warrior is as good as a Creek. I emerged from the combat with honor, and it did not take long for my adventure to be generally known. . . ."

A few days later MacGillivray said to him that if, as it appeared, he had no insurmountable objection to Indian women, he might marry MacGillivray's own sister, who spoke English and who would be a useful interpreter. And so it was done, and Milfort was bound to the nation by bonds of love and duty.

Ere long he was drawn into the savages' military councils. His own training served to suggest many devices of European strategy, new in the southern backwoods and effective against Indian enemies. He once saved the Creek army entire. He was made Little War Chief and at length, in an imposing ceremony, Great War Chief, or Tastanegy (Tustenuggee, according to Creek purists). In time of war he outranked even MacGillivray.

The Creeks were now allied with the English against the colonists. But the Tastanegy was given pause, prevented from smiting the young United States, by the news that the French had become the Americans' allies. He could not bring himself to fight the allies of his own countrymen.

He found an ingenious evasion of the dilemma. He took two hundred of his braves on a tour to see the homes of their ancestors.

It was an extraordinary journey. The party visited Mobile, "a little terrestrial paradise"; Pascagoula, the home of lazy but happy people; and New Orleans. The expeditionaries continued westward to the land of the Attacapas, falsely termed cannibals (they merely roasted Spaniards; they did not eat them); north to the land of the Nachitoches, a very gentle people who love the French very much; upstream along the Red River to the great caverns, the former home of the Creeks. Firing his gun in the caverns, Milfort startled more than four thousand bisons, who rushed out wildly and jumped to their death over a precipice into the Red River. In these ancestral caves the party wintered. Thence they marched hundreds of leagues south-southwest until they struck the Missouri River, a noteworthy feat, since the Missouri lies directly north. Here they found a tribe of white Indians, speaking a language which sounded like Breton. "They gave me a sort of a book, written by hand in their language. . . . I have since shown this to some Europeans, who recognized that it was written in Welsh."

Their course made amazing zigzags and took them to New Madrid, back to the Missouri, then to the Ohio, and finally home again, eighteen months after their departure. All voted that they had had a wonderful trip. But to Milfort's annoyance, the Revolution was still going on. He ran up to Philadelphia in a vain effort to find a French dealer who might be given the monopoly of the Creek trade. The Revolution came to a welcome end; Milfort returned to the Creek country, having successfully avoided fighting his countrymen and their allies.

He accepted the post of commissioner of the king of Spain among the Creeks. He carried on a war against the Georgians; he proposed an alliance of all the Indians against the whites. He was, unfortunately, absent when MacGillivray was seduced by Washington's emissaries and persuaded to come to New York to sign a treaty with the United States. Had he been present, he would have prevented this lamentable lapse of MacGillivray's and its lamentable consequences. MacGillivray accepted the commission of brigadier general in the United States Army, and the subjection it implied. Washington offered the same rank to Milfort. "I sent back [his presents], thanking General Washington for the offer he was so kind as to make to me." On being pressed, however, Milfort did accept a thousand dollars. And MacGillivray gave him a handsome pair of epaulets, the gift of Washington, who had had them from the king of France by the hand of Lafayette. Milfort later wore them in Paris. I can almost hear him. "Yes, they *are* nice epaulets. Rather a story connected with them. It seems that. . . ."

He made another long journey, with only a few warriors for companions. He visited Niagara Falls, the land of the Iroquois and the Hurons, Lakes Ontario, Erie, and Superior, and the Lake of the Woods. He returned down the Mississippi, through New Orleans. Somehow, he managed to see Vincennes, Indiana. The wine was poor there.

On his return to the Creek country, he learned that France and Spain were at war. He therefore resigned his post as Spanish commissioner. On receiving his passport he set out for France to persuade his countrymen to take Louisiana once more, by either diplomatic or warlike means. He offered the alliance of the Creeks to France. "I asked of France only a few men and little money. I answered for the plan's success."

Milfort bade the Creeks await his return and keep the peace till then. "I did not think my absence was to be so long. . . ." But then he learned that the Georgians were taking advantage of his absence to push into the Creek country! The Creeks remembered his injunctions. Meekly they suffered the affronts of the oppressor. They dared not take arms to ward off their own doom until their Tastanegy came again, as he had promised them. Such fidelity was equalled only by Casabianca.

So he left a post worth $3,500 a year in order to give France its great opportunity. He arrived in Paris in July, 1795; he saw Cambacérès and Treilhard, who were much impressed by his words. He interviewed the Directory, which accepted his plans, and opened negotiations with the court of Spain for the retrocession of Louisiana. Milfort was rewarded with the rank and pay of a *général de brigade*.

But when in 1800 Louisiana was ceded to France, Milfort found, to his horror, that he was overlooked. His *Mémoire*, written in haste (in three weeks, he said), is a statement of his extraordinary qualifications and a reminder to the government of its obligations toward him. With an air of respectful reproach he reveals the cause of the government's coolness; it is the calumnies of his enemies, the Americans. "Their overweening ambition tends to nothing less than to dominate the whole continent of America. . . . They know perfectly well that if the French government should permit me to put into effect the plans I have presented to it, their projects of aggrandizement would straightway vanish, and the nation of the Creeks which they take it on themselves to civilize would become for them a Medusa's head. And so they go to any length to destroy me in the minds of the government; they represent me as a man of no importance, helpless; they announce that I have no credit over the minds of the savages; that I am not their chief. . . ."

Here, at last, is the truth. The Americans were taking an

interest in him, obtaining damning reports from Georgia. Robert Livingston, ambassador to France, wrote to Secretary of State Madison, on March 24, 1802: "There is a man here who calls himself a Frenchman, by the name of Francis Tatergem [Tastanegy? or perhaps Tartarin?], who pretends to have great interest with the Creek nations. He has been advanced to the rank of General of Division. He persuades them that the Indians are extremely attached to France, and hate the Americans; that they can raise 20,000 warriors, that the country is a paradise, etc. I believe him to be a mere adventurer; but he is listened to, and was first taken up by the old Directors."

His enemies, the Americans, were checking up. We seem to be still checking up. But I am not your enemy, General; I am really very fond of you. I am a party to no conspiracy.

Still, I must check up on your recollections by the testimony of others. And this is the best I can find:

Milfort was reported by the Spanish to have come to the Creek nation in 1785 (Arthur P. Whitaker, "Alexander MacGillivray," *North Carolina Historical Review*, 1928). He was a Spanish agent among the Talapuche Indians (*Annual Report, American Historical Association*, 1896). An American agent referred to him, on May 7, 1794, as "one Milford" (*U.S. State Papers, Indian Affairs*). To say "one Milford" is to say an insignificant fellow, no Tastanegy. Another agent beat about no bushes. He wrote: "That rascal, Melford, is at the Tuckaubtachees." He said that Milfort was ready to betray the Spanish. "Even Melford, their great Colonel, has taken miff at their putting one over him" (*U.S. State Papers, Indian Affairs*). The United States placated with money and gifts the influential chiefs of the Creeks, the Mad Dog of the Tuckabatchees, the Hollering King, Old Red-Shoe, King of the Alabamas. But there was never any mention of Tastanegy Milfort.

MacGillivray had only two sisters, Mrs. Durant and Mrs. Weatherford. There was none to marry Milfort (Benjamin

Hawkins, in *Georgia Historical Collections*). The record of his tremendous journeys is simply impossible. The tales of his military eminence in the nation are merely lies. His book is mostly lies.

His book is not, however, without value. His descriptions of backwoods life, of Indian customs and ceremonies, have the sound of authenticity; they are soberly regarded by modern anthropologists (John R. Swanton, *Early History of the Creek Indians;* Albert S. Gatschet, *A Migration Legend of the Creeks*).

And we must not lightly say that even lies are without value. Is it so clear that interesting lies are less to us than dull truths? Is the process of extracting truth from lies less important to the historian than that of extracting lies from truths?

From Milfort's maltreatment of truth and from the references of others we can draw some confident conclusions.

The mysterious period of his life dates from 1774 to 1785. He found it advisable in his *Mémoire* to account, in mendacious detail, for his occupations during those years. He seems to be trying to throw his superiors off the scent. Indeed, it must have been something pretty distressing that would send a French soldier, under a new name, to the Gulf Coast of America and the service of the king of Spain. From 1785 to 1795 we know that he was Spanish agent among the Indians. As such, he could live that life of hunting, sloth, drunkenness, and brawling which satisfies many natures, even those of some contemporary country gentlemen. Major Caleb Swan, whom Milfort claimed to know well in Alabama, but who fails to mention Milfort, says: "The whites living among the Indians (with very few exceptions) are the most abandoned wretches that can be found, perhaps, on this side of Botany Bay; there is scarcely a crime but some of them has been guilty of" (Caleb Swan, in H. R. Schoolcraft, *Indian Tribes*).

When Milfort learned, probably in 1793, that Spain and the French republic were at war, he saw his great opportunity.

With luck, he might persuade the French government to put him in command of an army to conquer Louisiana for France, with the aid of his Creek friends. We have seen that his proposal was for a time taken seriously by the Directory. His assumed title as Tastanegy of the Creeks brought him the genuine commission of general in the army of France.

His *Mémoire* must be regarded as a *pièce justificative* in his campaign. It is designed to prove to doubting ministers his intimate knowledge of the Indians, from Canada to the Gulf, his familiarity with the whole Mississippi territory, his power over the savages, his own popularity and that of the French among them, his long fidelity to France, the importance of the Mississippi trade, and the growing menace of the United States. Unfortunately, such doom is over us when we take pen in hand, he must have revealed to the ministers that he was a liar, a braggart, and a fool.

He was given no chance to put his project into effect. Nor was he permitted to serve according to his rank in the French army, else we might have had Creek tactics in European meadows, the Tuckabatchee war whoop at Waterloo. He wreaked his ill humor on his wife. A European, it would seem, she endured the kicks and contumely of an Alabama squaw. She brought suit for separate maintenance; the fiery general avoided the payments, first by defying the ministry and then by dying, on August 12, 1819.

A terrible fellow, his wife would have told us, on whom we should waste none of the favor we so unreasonably confer on the scapegraces of the past. A terrible fellow, certainly; heaven preserve us from ever having to do with his like. And yet there is this much to be said for him: he is perhaps the only general of the French army who obtained his commission and retained it by barefaced lying. And he wrote a very interesting and amusing book. Now that most of his virtuous contemporaries have had virtue's reward, oblivion, General Milfort still palely lives on in the minds of those who occasionally read his book, and those who even occasionally read sober articles in solemn books.

The Duc de Montpensier made this sensitive double portrait of himself and his brother Louis Philippe (left) five years after their visit to the United States

13 King Louis Philippe in the U.S.A.

Louis Philippe, Duc d'Orléans, destined to be king of the French from 1830 to 1848, spent more than three years in American exile, from 1796 to 1800. Greedily curious, he and his two younger brothers traveled many thousands of miles in the United States, from Maine to New Orleans. The original record of their journey, long vainly sought, was discovered in 1955 when Mme Marguerite Castillon du Perron gained access to the Orléans family papers in the strong room of Coutts's Bank, London. Locked in that grim prison, she found an autograph travel journal of the future king. The substance of the record she reported in her *Louis-Philippe et la Révolution Française* (1963). The information she provides, added to our previous knowledge and many local memories, permits us to reconstitute the noble gentlemen's adventures.

The dukes of Orléans, Princes of the Blood, were cousins of the Bourbon kings. For a century and a half they stood, impatient, on the lower steps of the throne, as the Bourbons produced many daughters and few sons, and those sickly, early to quit the world. By 1790 Louis Philippe Joseph, Duc d'Orléans, counted only five male Bourbons between him and the royal seat.

In the Revolution he proclaimed himself a liberal, courted popularity, and, rechristened Citoyen Egalité, voted in the *Convention*, in January, 1793, for the execution of King Louis XVI. But liberalism could not save him; he too was guillotined in the same year, hated alike by the radicals as a rich patrician and by the world's gentlefolk as a regicide and fratricide. All his accessible property was confiscated.

Philippe Egalité had displayed his advanced views in the education of his three sons. They were put in the charge of a remarkable woman, Mme de Genlis, poet, novelist, musician, and theorist of education according to the doctrines of Rousseau. The boys learned by doing, by games and dramatizations. At lunch they talked only English, at dinner, Italian. They absorbed botany and German by tending their own garden plots under the eye of a monoglot German gardener. They were toughened by sports, by wearing lead-soled shoes on long walks, by sleeping on the floor with a single blanket, by carrying their own washing water to the top floor of their château. They worked with the peasants in vintage time and practiced manual trades. Louis Philippe, the eldest, was an excellent cabinetmaker, and proudly constructed an armoire and a table with sweetly sliding drawers. He learned the elements of medicine from a surgeon and served for a time as a hospital orderly. This was an education not only for the life of privilege; it was an education for adversity, an education of foreboding. The governess "brought us up with ferocity," remembered Louis Philippe; and she: "He was a prince and I made him a man, slow and I made him clever, a coward and I made him brave; but I could not make him generous."

Louis Philippe, sixteen at the outbreak of the Revolution in 1789, joined the left-wing Jacobin Club and the freethinking Masons. He entered the army as a colonel, and as lieutenant general fought well in battles against the coalition of European powers. But the excesses of the Paris terrorists and the guillotining of King Louis XVI revolted him; in April, 1793, he fled to the Austrian lines. He was universally distrusted, by the republicans as a renegade, by the royalists as an ex-Jacobin and son of the infamous Philippe Egalité. He was in danger; he was also nearly penniless, though the son of once the richest man in France. He took refuge in Switzerland under an assumed name, and with a faithful manservant, Baudoin, made a walking tour, sleeping often in barns and eating what country food the two could afford. He found a post teaching French and mathematics in a Catholic school at Reichenau. He also busied himself getting the cook with child and was discharged, not so much for his offense against morality as for causing the breakdown of the school kitchen.

He had to wander on. Collecting some of his father's funds from London, in 1795 he made with the devoted Baudoin a journey to Lapland and the North Cape, a very unusual tourist trip in his time. He was sheltered briefly by a missionary and left his host's sister-in-law with a royal souvenir, male.

He spent the winter in Germany, under various aliases, while his mother negotiated a deal with the French Directory. His younger brothers, the Duc de Montpensier and the Duc de Beaujolais, were imprisoned in Marseilles. The Directory wanted them out of the way, but not necessarily dead; the vogue of the guillotine had passed. The Directory engaged to release the brothers if they would intern themselves, with Louis Philippe, in America. The arrangement was made, though there was a little money difficulty. Gouverneur Morris, who had been American minister to France, came to the rescue with an advance of $4,000 to Louis Philippe, and later increased his loan to $13,000. (The debts were repaid with interest in 1816 and 1818, when the Orléans fortunes had turned.)

Passing as a German merchant, Louis Philippe and the faithful Baudoin—the two younger brothers were to follow later—sailed from Hamburg on the *America* and arrived in

Philadelphia on October 23, 1796. The shipowner, David Conyngham, learned the passenger's identity and offered him temporary hospitality. He did not lose a moment in informing Philadelphia society of his distinguished guest. Hearing the report, Miss Lucy Breck informed her diary that a real prince had arrived in the republican city! She immediately commanded a new dress. And on the twenty-eighth she wrote: *"I have seen him* and yet I live! He is rather tall, and pretty well formed; but none of that commanding dignity, or even ease of manner, which is generally looked for. . . . There was, however, a degree of modesty, united to the appearance of a good understanding, discovered in his Countenance." A most amiable character, she summed up; but evidently he was not quite a Prince Charming.

On the other hand, his easy, friendly manners commended him to the merchant aristocracy of Philadelphia. Lucy's father, Samuel Breck, said: "Amiable and unpretending in conversation and general conduct, ever cheerful and apparently forgetful of his lost rank, he conformed his demeanor to that of our own manners in our best-bred Circles, and was everywhere treated with distinguished regard." John Pickering called him "plain but intelligent, of good person and deportment." Others speak of his maturity, good sense, good nature, modesty, and simplicity of manners. He lodged in a single room. Baudoin did the shopping; his hard bargains were remembered for years by the market women. Louis Philippe was unabashed. He gave a dinner for some distinguished guests, among them John Singleton Copley, Jr., son of the painter and future Lord Chancellor of England. He sat half his guests on the bed, remarking that he had himself occupied less comfortable places without the consolation of such an agreeable company. In short, he put on the democratic character of his companions, as he could put on the character of a schoolmaster or a frontiersman. This adaptability was to serve him later, when he became *le roi bourgeois*, going shopping with his queen in the Paris stores and taking his purchases home in the omnibus, and carrying an umbrella instead of a sword.

There was one quality the Philadelphia merchants could readily appreciate. He was extremely close, if not stingy, and had been so from childhood despite Mme de Genlis' correction. The Comte de Neuilly, who knew him as a boy, recalled that he would ask the price of everything, meditate, and end by saying: "*C'est cher! C'est trop cher!*" His parsimoniousness had developed in his years of near-destitution in Switzerland and Lapland. During his American travels he kept close account of all his expenditures. The habit persisted when he sat on the French throne. It is said that he checked grocer's bills, sold his candle ends, had the royal table supplied by a restaurateur at four francs a plate. The leftovers were served in a cheap eating house in the Palais-Royal.

In Philadelphia, of course, he was entertained by all the great families: the Binghams, the Robert Morrises, the Willings, the Cadwaladers, the Chews. He painted a miniature of Miss Abby Willing, and is said to have offered her his hand; and her father is said to have pronounced sententiously: "As an exile, destitute of means, you are not a suitable match for my daughter. Should you recover your rights, she will not be a suitable match for you." He attended the inauguration of President Adams. He watched Gilbert Stuart at work on a portrait of Washington. And ever he awaited the promised arrival of his two brothers.

They came at length on February 8, 1797, after a long crossing on a dirty Swedish ship, the *Jupiter*, chartered by the American government to bring home eighty Americans redeemed from slavery in Algiers. The reunion, Louis Philippe said later, was the happiest day of his life. The Duc de Montpensier, now twenty-one, was thin, wispy, and melancholy, yellow-haired, dark-eyed, with a sensitive face. He was delicate and fastidious; he detested wine and, much more, American whisky. His great love and solace was art. He was an excellent painter by any reckoning, and would have some standing in art history today had he not been a prince and had not most of his works been destroyed in the sack of the royal palaces in 1848. The second brother, the Duc de Beaujolais, was only seventeen. He was undersized, "almost a dwarf," said one scornful observer. But after all, he had just spent in prison four years proper for growth. Others call him strongly built, bright, witty, very good-natured, and even "a beautiful youth." The brothers brought their faithful dog, companion of their prison life. His race and name have not been recorded.

Though Louis Philippe took for the brothers a house at the northwest corner of Fourth and Prune streets, they did not linger long in Philadelphia. Louis Philippe, that earnest tourist, was eager to explore the backwoods of America, to confront the virtuous uncorrupted savages, to inspect such natural wonders as Niagara Falls. He may also have thought that a little toughening, à la Mme de Genlis, was just what his brothers needed. He may even have wished to demonstrate to Miss Abby Willing, by a plunge into the wilderness, the romantic consequence of a broken heart.

The brothers rode away late in March, 1797, accompanied by good Baudoin and the nameless dog. Louis Philippe noted that the four horses cost $130, the gear $70. Mr. Samuel Breck (and Miss Lucy?) saw them off, and observed that they had adopted the style and dress of western traders, that is, deerskin breeches and long, loose frocks of linsey-woolsey or deerskin, belted to make a pouch at the breast for provisions. But in their saddlebags they carried white satin suits with lace ruffles, in which to appear, at need, with decency.

They took the Baltimore road through "a swampy and dreary country." They stopped at roadside inns, registering as Mr. Orleans, Mr. Montpensier, and Mr. Beaujolais. In Baltimore they broke out their satin suits to dine with Richard Caton, General Samuel Smith, and the rich merchant Robert Gilmor, who kindly presented them with a letter of credit.

On April 3 the party reached Washington, "a city laid out upon paper, staked out in swamp-land." One wing of the new Capitol rose in the midst of desolation. Louis Philippe was not impressed. He found the President's House (only the shell of the present White House) mean and heavy, with a ridiculously small entrance. (This defect was in fact corrected after the British burned the building in 1814.)

Two days later the travelers, delayed by the necessity of having their laundry done, presented themselves at Mount Vernon. The flustered Negro doorman reported to General Washington: "Your Excellency, there are three Equalities at the door!" The General received them with his usual courtly grace. They talked late that evening, chiefly about the institution of slavery, a subject that fascinated Louis Philippe. He was inclined to foresee a bloody slave rebellion, like that of Santo Domingo. Mount Vernon, to be sure, presented an example of a model plantation, with the slaves apparently contented. But Baudoin, who gained the confidence of the house servants, reported that they longed for freedom, even without contentment, and envied fugitives to the North.

The following morning the brothers rose at six thirty and, looking out the window, perceived their host returning from an inspection of his lands. "Do you get along without sleep?" Louis Philippe asked at breakfast. "I always sleep well," he replied, "for I never wrote a word in my life which I had afterwards cause to regret."

They announced to the General their purpose of exploring the mysterious interior of America. He was much interested; he took a copy of Abraham Bradley's recent map of the United States and on it traced in red ink a recommended itinerary. Years later King Louis Philippe liked to impress American visitors by unfolding his map and pointing to the red line drawn by the hand of the great Washington.

After four happy days at Mount Vernon, the party set out to follow Washington's guideline. At Leesburg they were interrupted at dinner by Colonel Burgess Ball, Washington's cousin, who insisted on carrying them off to his plantation and boring them through a long evening. "Boredom and wasted time," Louis Philippe noted in his journal. "The only thing I am interested in is the aspect of the country, the state of agriculture and that of the houses and inhabitants."

The travelers entered the rich valley of the Shanadore, or Shenandoah. At Winchester they stopped at the inn of Mr. Busch, originally from Mannheim. Louis Philippe conversed familiarly with him in German, then requested that they be served in their room, since one of the brothers was indisposed. But Mr. Busch exclaimed in outrage: "If you are too good to eat at the same table with my other guests, you are too good to eat in my house! Begone!" And, indeed, they were driven forth in a storm of rain and hail, to push on eighteen miles to Strasburg and to meditate on the peculiarities of democracy.

The brothers followed the "Great Indian Warpath," now placid Route 11, through Harrisonburg, Staunton, Lexington, Salem, and so southwest into Tennessee. The well-traveled road was tolerable enough, the food—salt pork and hoecake—revolting, the inns frightful. But they apparently succeeded in dodging Mrs. Tease's tavern, near Staunton, which the Marquis de Chastellux ten years before had described as "one of the worst in all America. . . . A solitary tin vessel was the only bowl for the family, the servants, and ourselves. I dare not say for what other use it was proposed to us on our going to bed." On this theme, Louis Philippe asked one evening for a chamber pot; the hostess pointed expressively to a glassless window.

To Louis Philippe most of the land seemed monotonous, endless forests wherein even the birds were mute. But wild turkeys, partridges, blue pigeons, and deer abounded. Although the travelers were well received in the rare homes of gentry, they found most of the human inhabitants unwelcoming. "Nothing can equal the shiftlessness and disobligingness of the workers here. When a horse needs shoeing one must sometimes travel twenty-five miles before getting aid, and one must call on five or six farriers before finding one who is willing to work. If anything happens to a saddle, a coat, or a boot, one finds no one to repair it. The other day a cobbler said to us: 'Yes, I'm a cobbler. I work sometimes, but now I don't feel like it.'"

The brothers crossed into the new state of Tennessee and arrived on April 30 at its capital, Knoxville, consisting of about a hundred houses. Though their inn was a good five years old, the bedroom walls still gaped where the builders had withdrawn the beams supporting the scaffolding. Modern research identifies their stopping place as Chisholm's Tavern, still standing, and records a tradition that Louis Philippe, assailed by bedbugs, greased himself vainly with hog's lard and finally ran out screaming to plunge into the Tennessee River.

Here the travelers made a digression to visit the Cherokee reserve in the Great Smokies, around Tellico Plains, sixty miles south of Knoxville. The Indian agents and a small garrison occupied a fort, or blockhouse, which commonly stood wide open. Indians strolled in, picked up pipes lying about, squatted, and smoked. The fort contained a store where white men's goods—but no whisky—were for sale at nominal prices. Indian produce was similarly cheap. Louis Philippe, always delighted with a bargain, bought a pig, a wild turkey, and a gallon of strawberries for a quarter-dollar. The commander, Major John Strother, was proud of his peaceable kingdom. He explained that the famous Indian atrocities were usually reprisals for the atrocities of aggressive whites trying to provoke government intervention and the confiscation of Indian hunting grounds.

The princes visited the Indian village, of which the chief feature was the *maison de ville*, or town hall, a large hexagonal structure, log-framed, roofed with cornstalks and resembling an enormous haystack. It was used for meetings and for ritual dance. Three pillars supported tribal totems—snake, tortoise, lizard—painted in black on white panels and reminiscent of coats of arms.

Louis Philippe, ever curious, inquired into the Indians' religion (they seemed to do without), legal system (they made laws readily and as readily forgot them), division of labor between the sexes, status of women, sexual morality (it barely existed). He noted that the promiscuity of the women deprived them of male respect. He drew a lesson for France: the new laws permitting freedom of divorce will bring in something like Indian concubinage. Women, he wrote, can rise out of their present dependence "only by the sentiments they inspire in men, not at all by the pleasures they may offer. To avoid debasement these pleasures should be reserved, as a means of augmenting the emotions of the lover who thinks himself beloved. But if the pleasures are lavished on many, the magic of emotion disappears, and women fall into debasement and thence into dependence."

With the commandant's permission, Louis Philippe offered a prize of two kegs of whisky to induce the Indians to stage a ball game, beside what is still known as Ball Play Creek. The contestants, their bodies oiled, tried to drive a deerskin ball between the opponents' goal posts. All means of propulsion were permissible: feet, hands, and short lacrosse sticks. The spectators admired the players' agility and ferocity.

The next day, disregarding an Indian deputation that presented the empty whisky kegs and asked for a refill, the travelers returned north and headed west for Nashville. They now entered a difficult, debatable land, where the Indians were still unpacified. They were adjured by white settlers to join an armed party, but they were too impatient and reckless to delay. The road was a mere track through the wilderness. There was not a settler for a hundred miles; and when at length the wayfarers found one, he had no food for sale except a little smoked bear's grease and corn. The track is followed by modern Route 70 and 70N, across Crab Orchard Gap, through the present Crossville and Cookeville to Carthage on the Cumberland River. The river was then bordered by nearly impenetrable cane brakes. Cabins and tilled fields began to appear. At Major Dickson's in Castalian Springs the Frenchmen had their first coffee in many a day.

On May 10 they arrived in Nashville, a town of some eighty houses, with pretensions toward elegance. An English visitor in this year was astonished to see there two coaches "fitted up in all the style of Philadelphia or New York." The princes stopped at Captain Jesse Maxwell's house, now the Maxwell House Hotel. They had envisioned relative comfort, after their nights under the stars or the rain. But court was in session and the inn crowded; they were forced to sleep three in a bed. (Later King Louis Philippe liked to ask Americans: "Do they still sleep three in a bed at Nashville?") They met some of the town's celebrities, including Captain Timothée de Montbrun, a former French officer turned Indian trader, who on meeting the princes was "excited like one affected with St. Vitus' dance; he could not keep his hands, his feet, or his tongue still."

Now the party turned north, on a track or "trace" that has become Route 31E, through Gallatin and Glasgow. They passed through the "Barrens," a wild, hungry, treeless land, almost empty of settlers. They stopped one night at a Captain Chapman's; he greeted them with suspicion, presuming their purpose to be the rousing of the Indians against the Americans. The captain was an angry man; he asserted that all the West hated the American government, the worst conceivable. Night fell; the captain and his wife took a "puncheon" bed of trimmed timber at one side of the room, "that seemed to us very natural." The Frenchmen disposed themselves on the floor, with their feet toward the fire. Another bed stood beyond them. "A rather pretty girl, whom we knew to be unmarried, got into it; that also seemed very natural. A stalwart young man of twenty or twenty-two arrived soon afterward, as we were rolling up in our blankets, and without ceremony got into the girl's bed. Although this was certainly very natural, it caused us some surprise. It had no such effect on the captain, who, to repose himself from his day's labors, began a conversation of which we were the subject. He thought we were very queer folk to leave our home and endure all the fatigues of a hard journey in order to see wildernesses, savages and a thousand other things which he had good reason to find unworthy of such efforts. The familiar behavior of the young man with the girl did not seem to upset him. His other daughter blew out the candle and got into the young people's bed, so that the youth was between the two girls. That seemed fairly extraordinary to us, but the matrimonial conversation went on without a pause."

Riding through pouring rain, fording swollen rivers, suffering often from hunger, the princes reached Hodgenville, and, according to local tradition, were well entertained by the proprietor, Mr. Hodgen. (In a cabin a few miles away Abraham Lincoln would be born twelve years later.)

Thus they came to Bardstown, a metropolis of a hundred and fifty houses. Louis Philippe was ill; he asked the landlady for some special attentions. These were refused, for an Irishman in a clown costume was parading the town and announcing a puppet show. There had never been any public amusement in Bardstown, and the entire staff of the inn would attend the show. The hostess took all her children, "so that when they are old they will be able to say they have seen it."

The Bardstown Catholic church, once a cathedral, still proudly displays a collection of paintings, allegedly by Murillo, Rubens, van Eyck, Van Dyck, etc., said to have been given later by King Louis Philippe in gratitude for his warm reception in the village. It is hardly necessary to remark that Louis Philippe would not have given anyone a million dollars' worth of art, and least of all Bardstown. There is, however, some reason to suppose that the church clock was his gift.

It was in Bardstown that he wrote (on May 21) the last entry in his journal, summing up his impression of the Kentuckians: "What makes a journey in this region absolutely unendurable is the character of the new settlers. They are the lowest sort of men I have ever seen. In general they are the scum of Ireland and the United States. They are coarse, idle, and inhospitable to the utmost degree. Nothing is more disgusting than to see such people continually. I must admit that, despite my prejudice against the Irish settlers, I have always found them more hospitable and less disagreeable than the American settlers. Altogether, I don't think that in any corner of Europe one could find such a degraded lot."

This opinion is supported by the Englishman Thomas Ashe, who visited Bardstown in 1806. "Of the inhabitants I have already said enough to make humanity shudder. They trample on all the advantages spread before them by nature, and live in a brutal ignorance of the charms and luxuries which surround them." Poor Mr. Ashe was particularly revolted by the Kentuckians' diet. "They eat salt meat three times a day, seldom or never have any vegetable, and drink ardent spirits from morning till night. They have not only an aversion to fresh meat, but a vulgar prejudice that it is unwholesome. The truth is, their stomachs are depraved by burning liquors, and they have no appetite for anything but what is highly flavored and strongly impregnated with salt." (In our glorification of the bold pioneers we forget that they were commonly regarded as outcasts of civilization, too indolent and incompetent to survive in the settled country. O pioneers! There were heroes among you; there were also derelicts and outlaws.)

Now the road turned east, to Lexington, the trading center of the Kentucky country. Somewhere on the way Louis

Philippe must have paused to tend his illness, for the stage of the journey from Bardstown to Pittsburgh, something over three hundred miles, occupied a month. The road was the main access to the Kentucky country from the northeastern states and was relatively good. The princes crossed the Ohio River at Maysville. In Chillicothe, Ohio, Louis Philippe intervened in a barroom brawl and rescued the landlord. His role was always to be that of a peacemaker. In Zanesville he lodged in the cabin of John McIntire, who is remembered in Muskingum County as "of a pleasant disposition except when insulted, when he would instantly knock the offender down, and go off about his business." Thence the travelers headed east, through Wheeling, and arrived in Pittsburgh on June 20.

Here they rested for several days. They were cordially received by the great men of Pittsburgh, including General John Neville and Hugh Henry Brackenridge, author of *Modern Chivalry*. Neville's son was impressed by the brothers' familiar, democratic manners, and by Beaujolais' playfulness. He remembered Louis Philippe as rather taciturn, melancholy, and subject to fits of abstraction. Of course, he may have been suffering from the sequels of illness. The visitors made friends with the picturesque émigré the Chevalier Dubac, who was described as "the most popular citizen of the village." Though once an attaché of the French legation in Constantinople, he was not at all cast down by ill fortune. He opened a *confiserie*, making a specialty of burnt maple sugar, peach-flavored, with hazelnuts and walnuts. He had a pet monkey, Sultan, who he insisted could tell counterfeit money from genuine. "Allons, Sultan," he would say, "tell dese good ladie de good money from de counterfeit." After some byplay, Sultan would scrape all the money into the cash drawer. "Madame, he is like de Pope; he is infallible."

From Pittsburgh the course led north to Erie, Pennsylvania, then east along the shore of Lake Erie. Ever curious about the natives, Louis Philippe paused at the Cattaraugus Reservation of the Seneca Indians. Here, apparently, occurred an incident that always amused the younger brothers. The chief was ill; Louis Philippe prescribed and performed a bleeding. Much relieved, the chief granted the medicine man his highest mark of esteem; he installed the visitor for the night in the place of honor, between the chief's grandmother and his great-aunt. It is true that in the morning the chief tried to impound, by a legal quibble, the brothers' faithful, far-traveled dog.

Thus they came to Buffalo Creek, no more than an Indian trading post. They crossed to the Canadian side of the Niagara River and spent a day regarding Niagara Falls. Montpensier made of the famous view a sketch, from which he later developed an oil painting, now in the New-York Historical Society's collections.

East of Buffalo, the track led through swamplands, inhabited only by mosquitoes. Floundering through the wet woods, the Frenchmen met a party bound for Niagara, and recognized Alexander Baring, an Englishman who was engaged to the daughter of the great William Bingham of Philadelphia; she was the cousin of sweet Abby Willing. He found the princes wearing ragged clothes and gaping boots, and nearly penniless. He asked if the sight of Niagara was really worth all the toil and pains, and was assured that indeed it was. (Later, as Lord Ashburton, Baring was to reappear in American history as signer of the Webster-Ashburton Treaty.)

The princes emerged from the sloughs; Montpensier wrote to his sister: "We have spent fourteen nights in the woods, devoured by all kinds of insects, soaked to the skin, unable to get dry, eating pork and sometimes a little salt beef and cornbread." They crossed the Genesee at Avon Springs by Widow Berry's rope ferry and reached an outpost of civilization in Dr. Timothy Hosmer's sanitarium beside healing springs. Here they found excellent fare, and incredibly a bathhouse, and just as incredibly a well-chosen library. Their courtly host, a former surgeon in the Revolutionary army, was in local remembrance "a gentleman of the old school, scrupulously clean and neat, with a portly frame and erect military carriage. His hair was ribbon-tied, and carefully powdered by his black servant, Boston. His breeches of soft and nicely-dressed deerskin were fastened at the knees by silver buckles." It seemed to the princes that they were re-entering a lost world.

The impression was reinforced, a day's journey farther on, in Canandaigua. Here the bedraggled travelers were greeted in perfect French by Thomas Morris, son of the financier Robert Morris and agent for the newly opened lands of the Genesee country. He had been educated in France and had brought with him to these backwoods an accomplished French chef. He put up the visitors in his comfortable house, supplied all their wants, took them on fishing trips on beautiful Canandaigua Lake. They made friends with a young Scottish clerk in the land office, John Greig, and all, wearing moccasins, went hunting deer and wild duck.

Years later Greig, lawyer and bank president, revisited Europe. Timidly he sent up his card to the French king: "John Greig, late of Canandaigua, America." As an awe-struck Canandaiguan had it from Greig, "the recollections of early scenes rushed vividly upon the mind of the monarch; and, laying aside his royal state, he went quickly to the door, threw it open, and, expanding his arms, fervently clasped John Greig to his bosom." During a whole month, "John must sit by his side at dinner, play at chess and cribbage with him in his library, and ride by his side. . . . When he left the court of St. Cloud, it was, as John Greig afterward said, like tearing himself from the home of his youth, and the embrace of a father."

At Thomas Morris' urging, and under his guidance, the party visited the falls of the Genesee, stopping for the night at the log house of Orringh Stone, in the present Brighton,

Rochester's suburb. The two-story frame tavern that succeeded the cabin a year or two later is now jealously guarded by the Society for the Preservation of Landmarks in Western New York. The falls themselves, though a disappointment after Niagara, tempted Beaujolais to make a sketch, and later a painting.

Our city of Rochester was no more than a deserted shanty in a swamp. In the 1840's King Louis Philippe inspected in a Paris exhibition a giant plate-glass window; he was told that it was ordered by a dry-goods store in Rochester. "What! Can it be that that mud-hole is calling for anything of the sort?"

Back in Canandaigua, the party met Captain Charles Williamson, the "Baron of the Backwoods," agent for the vast Pulteney estate, extending from the Genesee country to the Finger Lakes, and builder of wilderness cities complete with theater and racecourse. At his suggestion, the horses, nearly foundered after their long journey, were sent overland by easy stages to meet their riders at Northumberland, Pennsylvania, while the travelers proceeded to Geneva. Here, on July 13, they stopped, certainly, at Captain Williamson's magnificent three-story hotel, erected in 1796 and still today sheltering guests in diminished splendor. Thence they paddled, or sailed, the length of Seneca Lake, and then, on foot, carried their packs twenty miles to Newtown, now Elmira. Here they bought a boat of some sort, no doubt a Durham boat, or flat-bottomed scow, and on it floated down the Chemung and the Susquehanna.

A few miles below Towanda they came to Azilum, that remarkable colony established by a group of French *émigrés* to offer a refuge to Marie Antoinette and her family. The princes are said to have stopped here. This is possible but unlikely, for Azilum was fiercely legitimist, and the sons of Philippe Egalité would hardly have been welcome.

They continued down the Susquehanna to Wilkes-Barre. They seem not to have met their horses, but to have made the last stage of their journey on hired steeds and in public conveyances. They arrived in Philadelphia on or about July 27. They had been four months on the way and had covered well over two thousand difficult miles. They settled, with great relief, into their own house.

But yellow fever raged in sultry Philadelphia, and the gentry had fled the city. Early in October the princes set forth again on their travels. They stopped in New York to cash a $3,000 letter of credit from Gouverneur Morris, then continued by sloop to Providence and by stagecoach to Boston. They lodged at the Hancock House, in Corn Court, just south of Faneuil Hall. Louis Philippe often cited the hostess, the future Mrs. William Brazier, as a model housekeeper. The travelers were received by Boston's great: Harrison Gray Otis, John Amory, and others. They pushed on to Portsmouth and were welcomed in the pleasant mansion of Senator John Langdon. They spent a week at the home of Mrs. Martine, on nearby Sagamore Creek. Then onward to visit General Henry Knox in Thomaston, Maine, and General Henry Dearborn (whose name is still sacred in Detroit and Chicago) at Pittston, near Gardiner on the Kennebec River.

This was the travelers' farthest north. They turned back to Boston, and put up with a French tailor, James Amblard, at the corner of Marshall and Union streets. The Union Oyster House, on the same site, claims to remember the royal visitor, but the Union Oyster House has been in business a mere 142 years. (Do not believe its story that Louis Philippe set up as a teacher of French; he was well in funds, and anyway he was not in Boston for more than a week.)

Back in Philadelphia at November's end, the brothers learned that the French Directory had deported their mother to Spain. They immediately determined to join her there, declaring: "She shall not remain sonless while we are alive!" But there was a difficulty: England and Spain were at war, and communications between America and Spain were cut off. The princes saw only one possibility—to make their way to New Orleans, then held by the Spanish, and embark on a Spanish blockade-runner. The prospect of a two-thousand-mile journey in winter weather could not discourage them.

They set forth, riding westward, on December 10, with good Baudoin; but we hear no more of the globe-trotting dog. On the way Beaujolais fell ill. Unwilling to delay, the brothers bought a cart for their transport. In Carlisle, Pennsylvania, their horses took fright and ran away, crashing their cart into a tree and throwing out the occupants. Louis Philippe, though briefly knocked insensible, applied first aid and spectacularly bled himself before an admiring group of citizens. The next day a committee waited upon him and proposed that he should remain in Carlisle as the town physician. After he had become France's monarch, Louis Philippe loved to tell this story, concluding: "Perhaps I should have lived happier as the Doctor of Carlisle than as King of the French!"

When the princes arrived in familiar Pittsburgh, ice was already forming in the Ohio River, threatening to cut off navigation. They bought a keelboat, a raftlike craft guided by men with poles and a steersman with a sweep-oar. They were in constant danger from floating ice, from the menace of shoals and snags, from thievish Indians and even more thievish rivermen. They grounded once for twenty-four hours, while crewmen and princes worked together to set the vessel free. They arrived at last in New Orleans on February 17, 1798, after two months on the river.

Five weeks later they sailed in an American brig for Havana. On the way they were boarded by a British frigate; its captain proposed to impress the passengers to serve as British seamen, but Louis Philippe assumed his most regal air, revealed himself as the Duc d'Orléans, and successfully threatened the captain with vague governmental reprisals.

Havana proved to be no steppingstone to Spain. After long delay the government ordered the brothers back to New Orleans. They dodged the order, slipped away to the Bahamas, and thence made their way to Halifax, where they were warmly received by the Duke of Kent, the father of Queen Victoria. Failing to find a passage abroad, they returned to New York and at last sailed for England, arriving there in February, 1800. Unable to join their mother in Spain, in England they remained. Montpensier died in 1807 of tuberculosis. Beaujolais suffered from the same disease; Louis Philippe bore him off to sunny Malta in 1808, but the young man died on his arrival there. And Louis Philippe went on to his great destiny.

The Bourbon Charles X was driven from the French throne in the revolution of 1830; Louis Philippe modestly accepted the title of King of the French in a constitutional, bourgeois monarchy. He wrote to the historian François Guizot in 1839: "My three years' residence in America have had a great influence on my political opinions and on my judgment of the course of human affairs." Clearly his experience of democracy in action, his contacts with men of every sort, wise and simple, gentle and brutal, served him well. He gave France eighteen years of peace and prosperity, but in the end his people wearied of them both. In 1848 the mob attacked the Tuileries; king and queen simply hailed a cab and drove off to their final exile in England.

Historians in following regimes have treated him hardly, scorning his concern with money, his unconcern with glory, even the comical pear-shape he eventually assumed. Louis Philippe was unkingly in his subjects' eyes, as he had seemed unprincely to Miss Lucy Breck in Philadelphia. But there have been many worse rulers of France, both before and after.

As for Miss Abby Willing, she married Richard Peters, a substantial Philadelphia burgher. Probably she was much happier in the environs of Rittenhouse Square than she would have been in the Tuileries.

After escaping from a Cartagena jail, Moses Smith and his fellow fugitives, Sherman and Lippincott, are rescued from their small rowboat by a schooner bound for Baltimore

11 Corporal Moses Smith
and the Liberation
of South America

oses Smith was a Huntington, Long Island, Smith, a likely lad,
put to the trade of a cooper. In the first days of the year 1806,
when he was just twenty, he made a fateful journey to Brooklyn
to visit his uncle. There he met a former schoolmate, Richard
Platt, who had an unsettling story to tell. He had just enlisted in
a corps of light-horsemen, he said, recruited to guard the mails
from Washington to New Orleans. He was bound for only a
year, but if he should reenlist, he would be rewarded with lands
from the United States, and a bounty of fifty dollars at the end
of each year. He was to have a very handsome uniform.

Moses Smith was envious. The prospect of a lifetime
coopering barrels in Huntington seemed, by comparison, dull.
But Richard Platt kindly offered to share his good fortune and
to take Smith to the recruiting agent, John Fink, butcher and
tavern-keeper, of New York.

Here begins a tale of adventure and misadventure set down
by Moses Smith in a small and angry volume, which was published in 1814 and of which few copies exist today.

The two young men made a good crossing to New York
on the ferry, which was notorious for its disasters, commonly

caused by stampeding cattle and drunken oarsmen. They dis-embarked at the Fly Market, at Water Street and Maiden Lane, and walked north to the Butchers' Arms, at Bowery and Bayard streets. Here a number of young men were gathered, under the jovial auspices of the host, Mr. Fink. He had authority, he said, from President Jefferson to raise a corps of smart, stout young men for the Mail Guard. He told of the charms of travel, of the fine horses, the handsome uniforms. He offered the privates fifteen and a half dollars a month.

After several days' reflection, Moses Smith returned to the Butchers' Arms, where he was persuaded, in the mingling fumes of eloquence and rum, to sign a sheet headed "Muster Roll for the President's Guard." He received an advance of fifteen and a half dollars, with orders to report to the ship *Leander*, which would carry the men to Alexandria, Virginia, whence they would be marched to Washington.

One of the recruits demurred. It was known that the *Leander* was an armed vessel, carrying on a hazardous trade with Santo Domingo. Fink admitted that she was bound thither but said she was only going for coffee, and insisted that she would stop at Alexandria before heading for the Caribbean. "He made the most positive protestations and assurances of good faith," Moses Smith wrote later in his book, "(and to use his own phrase) said he would give us all liberty to cut his throat, if we were deceived in the slightest degree, and pledged his honor, that we should not be three weeks on board at the very most."

The men were taken aboard the *Leander*, at anchor in the North River. Something about her, perhaps her excess of arma-ment, perhaps the hard-bitten renegades who swarmed her decks, alarmed the prospective guardians of the Washington mail. Richard Platt and probably others deserted. When Moses Smith confessed to Fink that he was of a similar mind, the butcher put paper, pen, and ink before him and asked for a specimen of his handwriting. The result so pleased Fink that he immediately appointed Smith a corporal. "It was the first prize I had ever had for my scholarship, and was so much the more seducing," Smith admits, with surly satisfaction.

The *Leander* sailed on February 2, 1806, with a score of Fink's recruits, but without Fink, the hearty entrepreneur, the dealer in meats and men. The *Leander* was a vessel of 187 tons, mounting eighteen guns, and so intolerably crowded that the men were ordered to throw their trunks overboard. The ship's cargo, not accounted for on her manifest, included muskets, blunderbusses, carbines, field pieces, cutlasses, and five tons of lead.

When the *Leander* had been several days at sea, a striking figure, in a red gown and slippers, appeared on the quarter-deck. He was stoutish, dark-visaged, with an air of authority. His nose was large and handsome; his gray hair, powdered, was gathered in a knot behind and tied with a ribbon. One of the recruits, James Biggs, reported in a letter to his family that the man had "strong grey whiskers growing on the outer edges of his ears, as large as most Spaniards have on their cheeks." He had a constant habit of picking his teeth. "It was whispered about," says Moses Smith, "that he was a great general, called Miranda, whose name had been celebrated; but it was new and strange to me: I had never heard him spoken of by the politicians of Huntington, and I remained as ignorant as before I heard it, though something more alarmed and astonished."

General Miranda was, in fact, already inscribed on Fame's tablets. A Venezuelan by birth, he had served in the Spanish army, had been a general in the army of the French Republic, and had been petted, in the ancient and modern senses, by Empress Catherine of Russia. The revolutions in the United States and Europe had urged him to free South America from the Spanish yoke. After years of intrigue, in France, England, and America, he converted to his design Colonel William S. Smith, son-in-law of John Adams and Surveyor of the Port of

New York, and Samuel G. Ogden, owner of the *Leander*, a speculative New York merchant. General Miranda had interviewed President Jefferson and Secretary of State James Madison, and reported to his friends that President and Secretary approved his purpose, applauding the cause of liberty and the confounding of tyrant Spain.

Only a few of Miranda's two hundred recruits were informed of his high design. Most of them, men of crooked fortunes, had enlisted for a vague but profitable enterprise. If they smelt a rat, they liked the smell. Fink's victims found themselves mocked by their companions and sternly ruled by the ship's officers. They submitted; they had no recourse. Perhaps there was enough adventure in them to quiet their alarms.

Some semblance of drill was conducted on the *Leander*'s cluttered decks. Corporal Smith and a score of butcher boys, recruited by Fink at the Butchers' Arms, were formed into the First Regiment of Light Dragoons. The armorer was busy repairing old muskets, pointless bayonets, and rusty swords. "This tinker has his hands full," wrote James Biggs in a letter home, "as our arms are none of the best, and seem to have been already condemned in some other service. Whoever purchased them for the expedition was either no judge of arms, or he has been kinder to himself than his employer." Carpenters made staves for the cavalrymen's pikes, tailors confected varied and brilliant uniforms. A printing press clacked steadily, turning out proclamations and manifestoes to the people of South America.

The *Leander* made no halt at Alexandria. She arrived at Jacmel, on the south coast of what is now Haiti, and proudly ran up her new flag of freedom: red, yellow, and blue, rainbow colors. Here Miranda lingered for six weeks, trying with little success to obtain recruits. By somewhat high-handed means, he gained possession of two small American trading schooners, the *Bee* and the *Bacchus*. Meanwhile the news of his expedition was spread to all the Spanish shores.

Moses Smith and about forty others were assigned to the *Bee*. Several, including our hero, attempted escape, but were betrayed, overcome, and severely punished. They had no zeal for South American liberty, no hatred of any enemy save John Fink. Says Smith, "Mr. Fink's guard for the Washington mail were much more desirous of freeing themselves than of freeing anyone else."

The three vessels, slow sailers, lumbered toward the Venezuelan coast and arrived on April 27 off Puerto Cabello. In the midst of preparations for a landing, two fast, well-armed Spanish cruisers appeared. The *Leander* engaged them for a brisk half-hour, then crowded on all sail and bore away, leaving the unarmed *Bee* and *Bacchus* to be boarded and taken by the enemy. The captain of the *Leander* later explained this abandonment as an effort to tempt the Spaniards from their prey, so that he might subdue them singly. But the excuse was never accepted by Moses Smith and his companions, who regarded themselves as babes thrown to the wolves to permit the parents' escape.

The prisoners were taken ashore, loaded with irons, and thrust into two small dungeons in the fortress of Puerto Cabello. To all the horror of all loathsome prisons was added the moist, miasmic tropic heat of the seaboard. In Smith's dungeon, the captors closed the few small holes that were intended to admit air and light. With a penknife that someone had secreted, the prisoners succeeded in cutting a hole in the door. All day and night they took turns putting their mouths to this orifice. One man died of suffocation; nearly all were sick; several, says a survivor, lost their hearing.

Two months later the men were tried. They had no jury and no defenders. Smith was examined, through a drowsy interpreter, by the lieutenant governor of Caracas. When he tried to tell of Fink's duplicity, his examiner found such a story of a civilized country quite incredible. Ten officers of the Army of Liberation were sentenced to be hanged and to have their heads exposed in various cities. Moses Smith and twenty-three others, soldiers and mechanics, were given ten years' imprisonment. Nineteen men, mostly sailors, were let off with a term of eight years.

The prisoners were paraded to watch the execution of their officers. It was a horrid business. The Negro hangman, proud before his audience, pushed each victim from the gallows top, then slid down the rope to perch on the swinging body and drum his heels on the breast. When all were hanged, the ropes were cut, the bodies fell, and the gleeful Negro severed the heads with a chopping knife. The jail-weak survivors were forced to stand and watch these deaths for seven and a half hours of a Venezuelan July.

The condemned men were sent to their permanent prison in Cartagena, hottest and most pestilential of Caribbean towns. Smith, with twenty-seven others, was confined in a large cell within the castle; it was at least lighter and airier than the dungeon at Puerto Cabello. Yet the men continued to suffer all the tortures of the foulest imprisonment: heat, starvation, disease, brutality, filth. Smith tells them all; they are worse than one's imagination would readily conceive.

But at least there was hope to live on, for the prisoners were permitted to send a petition to Congress setting forth their distresses and pleading for the intercession of the American government.

A year after their incarceration, they were visited by an American skipper, Captain Carson. He told them that shortly after the sailing of the *Leander*, the government had proceeded in the New York courts against Colonel Smith and Mr. Ogden for promoting an insurrection in a friendly nation. In a celebrated trial, the two pleaded that they thought they had the consent of President Jefferson. Most right-thinking New Yorkers hated Mr. Jefferson. The jury, said to have been packed with anti-Jeffersonians, acquitted the defendants, to indicate that they believed Colonel Smith and Mr. Ogden, and thought the President lied when he disavowed any approval of Miranda's expedition. Thus the jury put the President woefully in the wrong and censured, by implication, his encouragement of foreign adventures.

The prisoners' petition, coming to hand soon after this trial, was laid before a Congress distraught with politics. Like many another petition, it was rolled up tight and used as a club. The President's recommendation that immediate steps be taken to obtain the prisoners' release was defeated in Congress on the ground that such intervention would be an acknowledgment of complicity with Miranda and his designs. The vote was considered an excellent blow to the presidential prestige. The nation's sympathy was, however, with the prisoners. Captain Carson, on a second visit, brought them a sum of money, taken in a public collection, as well as letters from home.

Even before the receipt of this news, the captives had recognized that help would come only from themselves. They must escape. To do so, they must break through a thirteen-foot wall, rid themselves of their irons, and somehow find their way to freedom.

The walls were pierced by several narrow loopholes, four or five inches in diameter, used for the drainage and ventilation of the cells. These opened on an ancient moat, now dry and filled with rank growth. The prisoners determined to enlarge one of the loopholes to permit the passage of their wasted bodies. For tools they had only a shoemaker's hammer, which they used to flatten straw for the hats they made for sale, and several knives, obtained, no doubt, by bribery of the guards.

They found that the walls were built of soft stone, brick, and mortar, which could be crumbled by the hammer and dug away by the knives. They dared not work by daylight nor after "lights out" at 11 P.M. But in the early evening the workers would remove a concealing hammock and painfully enlarge the loophole. Meanwhile the others would walk about, clanking their chains loudly, and singing to the music of a fife, a flute, and a fiddle, bought with Captain Carson's remittances. "And as our jailer kept a tavern and sold provisions, fruit, brandy, and segars, we found the way, while our money lasted, to temper his austerity, and have toleration for our noise."

The strongest, those most spared by fever, would take turns thrusting themselves into the hole and tunneling like beetles eating through wood. Often a section of soft mortar would permit a rapid advance; then a hard stone would drive them almost to despair. The tunnelers' last act each night was to replace the rubbish, plastering it with lime which the prisoners had obtained for washing their clothes and as a preservative against fever. So carefully was the work done that the inspecting corporal often looked through the loophole, yet noticed nothing amiss.

Meanwhile the men were working on their irons. These consisted of shackles on the ankles, weighing about twenty-five pounds, connected by chains permitting a six-inch step. The men's legs had grown so thin that they could draw the anklets up to their knees, suspending the chain by a string around the neck. Hacking one of their knives into a saw, they worked on the shackle bolts until these were nearly cut through and could be broken by quick pressure. The shining incisions were filled with wax, colored with dirt and rust.

After seven months of toil, the breach needed only the final thrust to be complete. The prisoners drew lots for the order of going. A few remained behind, some from prudence, and two because they were too large for the hole. Each fugitive knocked off his shackles, wormed through the dungeon wall, and dropped into the ditch. The dungeon was midway in the city wall, which ran parallel to the sea beach. Keeping close to the wall, they crawled in the moon's shadow for about half a mile. Then Moses Smith, who was sick, sank down, unable to proceed. His companions missed him, stopped, and listened, but none dared to call. After a time they resumed their fumbling journey.

Two of them, Sherman and Lippincott, became separated from the rest, found an Indian canoe, crossed an inlet, and with money and pleas persuaded some poor folk to shelter them. Fifteen others blundered along the shore for about ten miles, till they happened on an old Spanish fisherman. He engaged, for the fifty dollars which was all their wealth, to hide them and to carry them on the following night to Indian territory. But next day he learned that the governor was offering a reward of ten dollars per head for the fugitives. When night came, he put the fifteen passengers in his boat, and as he drew near shore, bade them lie in the bottom. And when they touched the bank, they were met by fifty armed soldiers. They were returned to prison and were there put in the stocks, with their feet a foot higher than their heads. Nor, for three months, were they released from the stocks for any reason whatever except death.

When Moses Smith lost touch with his fellow-fugitives, he found himself in a tangled, salty swamp, whence he could see every movement of the sentinel on the city wall. Dogs came nosing and barking; patrols of horsemen passed within a few feet of him. All day he lay there, without food, without water. At nightfall, he determined to cross the inlet by wading and swimming. "I had just entered the water, when the dogs came flying to the bank, and barked so furiously that I could see the sentinel turn round and remain in a posture of observation, looking toward where I was. I had but one resource, which was to sink down until my chin was covered, and so remain till these pitiless animals should cease of their own accord. In this position I remained for a length of time, and then moved on gently till I got out of my depth; I attempted to swim, but had not strength, and was forced to turn back. All this time I was under the terror of meeting with an Alligator, by which, as well as with Sharks, I understood these creeks to be thickly infested. Having got back again, I sat down all dripping on the oozy ground."

That night Smith wandered, bewildered and delirious, into the suburb of Xiximani. There he was accosted by a man, who said in broken English: "How do you do, sir?" Encouraged by his kindly tone, Smith threw himself upon his mercy and begged him to carry a letter to Captain Sanford, an American sea captain whose ship had been taken and who was himself a prisoner at large. The sympathetic native agreed, and fed and sheltered Smith for the night.

Captain Sanford had often visited the prison and was already in touch with Sherman and Lippincott. He arranged for the three fugitives to be hidden in the jungle. A month later all four embarked in an Indian pirogue, dug from a hollow log. And after much exertion and many dangers, they were taken on board an American schooner bound for Baltimore.

Not yet were Moses Smith's distresses at an end. Arriving in Baltimore on December 17, 1807, he set out the next day, weak and debilitated as he was, to walk to New York. He had but ten shillings in his pocket. When he tried to tell his story and asked for charity, he was mocked with sneers that "such stories are good to tell some people." His blood, thinned by the tropics, had no warmth against the winter. He slept in barns, in his wet and frozen clothes. But somehow, homing like a dog, he found his way to the door of his father, who had removed to Brooklyn.

Once fed and relieved, he thought of vengeance. Taking a pauper's oath, he brought suit in the New York courts against his seducer, John Fink. Fink engaged a good lawyer, who had the case postponed repeatedly till three and a half years had gone by and Smith's witnesses were dead or out of the country. When the case was finally argued, Smith was non-suited, because he could not produce the muster roll to which, five and a half years before, he had signed his name. Fink's lawyer moved that the plaintiff should pay the costs and suggested that, in their default, he should be whipped, as the law provided. But this, at least, he escaped.

Of the prisoners remaining in Cartagena jail, several were freed by the intercession of friends with the king of Spain. A few escaped in 1809. An American merchant in Cartagena secured the release of eleven in 1810. The others died of disease or maltreatment.

As for General Miranda, though his expedition to free Venezuela came to nothing, he was invited to his country in 1810 by the revolutionary party, and ere long he became Venezuela's first dictator. But an earthquake, taken by the populace as a sign of divine displeasure, undid him. Deported to Spain, he died in Cádiz jail. His marble tomb stands in Venezuela's Pantheon, beside that of Bolívar. The Venezuelans had not, at last reports, obtained any remains to put in the tomb.

I cannot find what happened to Moses Smith.

The legend on his vest identifies Barthélemy Prosper Enfantin, dressed in the summer uniform that he designed for himself and the followers of his Saint-Simonian socialism.

15 Le Père Enfantin

Familiar enough in history are the mighty rulers who have attained godhead and commanded the worship of their subjects. Unique, however, is the case of Le Père Enfantin, who, after a stage as deity, became general manager of an important railroad.

Barthélemy Prosper Enfantin emerged from a humility suitable for the origin of divinity. He was born in Paris in 1796, the illegitimate son of an impoverished banker. A brilliant student, he gained entry to the Ecole Polytechnique, the government school of engineering. After only a year, in 1814, his course was interrupted by the fall of Napoleon. He became a wine merchant. His powers of persuasion proving remarkable, he explored sales possibilities in Germany, Switzerland, and Holland. He spent two years in St. Petersburg as an employee of a French banker, thus learning the ways of finance. With a group of radical French expatriates he learned also to cogitate loftily on political economy and social theory, the making of a new world through the overturn of the old. He returned to France, worked as a bank teller, and addressed proposals for fiscal reform to the government. And he became a convert to the theories of Saint-Simon.

Claude Henri de Rouvroy, Comte de Saint-Simon, was the founder of French socialism. A touching idealist who fought for liberty in the American Revolution, he demanded a total reorganization of society on a basis of economics. Production of goods should replace landholding, for "the social aim is to produce things useful to life." Industrialists should take the place of nobles; scientists, instead of churchmen, should direct society, with the well-being of the proletariat as their aim. His followers preached that the inheritance of wealth should be forbidden, the gold base of money abolished, women emancipated, and a kind of United Nations established. Saint-Simon proclaimed: "To each according to his capacities, to each capacity according to its works."

In 1825 Saint-Simon died, and Enfantin inherited his prophetic robe. He devoted himself to spreading and improving the master's doctrines. He helped found a newspaper, gave public lectures, and rented a dilapidated residence in the rue Monsigny, near the center of Paris. There a group of adepts lived; and there resorted the social-minded, the forward-lookers, and the merely curious. "The family in the rue Monsigny was like a glowing fire," remembered Louis Blanc, famous in the history of social reform. "Many among the audience listened with a smile on their lips, and raillery in their eyes; but after the orator had spoken for a while there would be one feeling among his hearers of astonishment mixed with admiration."

Enfantin's heady doctrine was in part economic. Labor should gain all its rights and own the means of production. Banks, founded by the idle for idlers, should be organized by and for workers. His doctrine was also social. Privileges of birth and wealth should be abolished; merit alone should admit to power. Communal life should succeed to family grouping. Scholars, the new rulers and priests, would suppress poverty-breeding competition, war-breeding nationalism, the excesses of individual initiative. Women, who are clearly the equals or the superiors of men, should be freed from their vows of obedience and fidelity, which lead only to oppression, adultery, and prostitution. Each sex should have absolute liberty to determine its own fate; temporary marriages should be as legitimate and holy as permanent ones. Finally, Enfantin's doctrine was a metaphysic and a religious faith. Men are in communion with one another, with the universe. Matter as well as spirit is divine; the flesh is holy. We shall transmigrate into better bodies and share in a future life, though personality will not persist. "The dead have no other tomb than the living." God, obviously, is neither male nor female; He-She is an androgyne. The Couple, merging self with nonself, is the sacred unit. It followed that Enfantin, *le Père*, must find *la Mère* to form the priest-couple. Their mating, to be a symbol of social union, would bring a new revelation.

Much of the history of Enfantin's movement consisted in the hunt for the Mother, the female messiah. She was sought afar, not only in France, but in Turkey, Egypt, and America. Many candidates appeared, but the Father was always obliged to announce, after testing, that this again was not his destined bride. While awaiting her, he could not accept the bonds of human marriage. The announcement brought grief particularly to Adèle Morlane, mother of his son. Enfantin treated both mother and son very badly, according to the standards of Christian society, which are outworn, to be sure.

Enfantin was a great preacher of his Word. Everyone mentions his personal beauty. He was tall, elegant, with light chestnut hair, fine features, and compelling eyes. He threw on all "a spell of enchantment," said Louis Blanc. In a speech he would ascend from a plane of actuality to an empyrean of poetic but cloudy imagination. He could send an audience into convulsive ecstasies. One enthusiast was filled with the Holy Ghost and prophesied incoherently. Some auditors fainted and were removed without interruption to the proceedings. A magistrate had a stroke at one of the meetings and died, fortunately leaving all his property to the movement.

The faithful acclaimed Enfantin as the Chief of Humanity, the Living Law, the successor of Moses, Jesus, and Saint-Simon. Said one: "Father, I believe in you as I believe in the sun!" Many distinguished visitors sat in the hall: the critic Sainte-Beuve, the father of Rosa Bonheur, the poet Heine (who dedicated a book to Enfantin). Berlioz came; Liszt played the piano for waltzing. The composer Félicien David was a total convert. John Stuart Mill and Thomas Carlyle wrote their approval from England.

Early in 1832 Enfantin's mother died, leaving him a good-sized house set in ample gardens and grounds in Ménilmontant, on the eastern outskirts of Paris. (The site is marked by the tiny rue des Saint-Simoniens.) Le Père, discouraged by a falling-out with another leader of the movement, announced that forty of the faithful, all male, would take up residence in Ménilmontant and there await the promised Mother. "I can no longer be the mother who cradles her children and soothes them gently with her caresses. You are men, and I am the Father of Men." All the chosen were obliged to take a vow of chastity. Some indignant wives forced defections from the forty; other were left destitute with their children. But most of the adepts submitted to the divine command and declared their marriages void.

The Father designed a uniform for his apostles—white trousers in summer (blue in winter), a red-bordered white vest that laced up the back (symbolizing man's need of a companion, even to dress him), a blue tunic, a floating scarf, and a red toque. Across Enfantin's breast was embroidered: LE PERE. Above the new home floated a flag with horizontal stripes of white, violet, and red, representing religion, science, and industry. The schedule was military—reveille at 5 A.M., lights out at 9:30 P.M. There were no servants, for domesticity was branded as a form of slavery. Everyone took his turn at the housework, to the amusement of Paris cartoonists. Courses were given in astronomy, geography, geology, and music; and all had a hand in preparing the new gospel, *Le Livre Nouveau*, which would fix the dogma and practice of the faith. (The book was never, in fact, published.) Enfantin happily indulged his taste for bold reforms. He changed the names of the weekdays: Monday became Saint-Simon; Saturday, Le Père; Sunday, La Mère, Mother's Day. He planned a New City, which would take the form of the human body—at the head, the temples and academies of priests and scholars; in the stomach, factories and workshops; in the legs, promenades and parks; at the feet, dance halls.

Throngs of visitors were attracted to the biweekly open house at Ménilmontant. All danced, sang the new hymns, listened to the moving but disturbing discourses of the Father. The authorities were alarmed, recognizing the workings of a revolutionary spirit.

Enfantin and his chief aides were charged with "outrage against public morality" and arrested. The trial was the delight of Paris. The Father asked to be defended by women lawyers; since none existed, he acted as his own counsel. After a vain attempt to hypnotize judges and jury with his powerful eye, he proclaimed that he was sent by God, who is father and mother of all. "My mission is not ended! God has not made incarnate his Word in man for a second time, only to crucify him again between thieves! God does not repeat himself!" Nevertheless the jury found him guilty; with two others, he was condemned to a year in jail.

He found his martyrdom very tolerable. He was comfortably lodged in a de luxe political prison. He collected a large library and had plenty of leisure for his literary work. The faithful loaded him with dainties. The warden even asked him to dine, but he refused on a point of etiquette, since the invitation arrived only half an hour before the function.

But on his release, in 1833, he found his movement tottering. Far from daunted, he proposed to visit Egypt: to find *la Mère*, to convert the Egyptians to Saint-Simonism, and to build a canal across the Isthmus of Suez. The project of a canal, already thousands of years old, appealed to the engineer in him. Since he saw things in the large, he announced as his purpose the reconciliation of the Orient and the Occident. But money for such a grandiose enterprise was lacking; it was barely sufficient for boat fare.

Enfantin and twelve followers, including some engineers, disembarked in Egypt in apostolic destitution. They were succored by the French colony and were presented to the pasha, who found their scheme of canal building terrifyingly expensive. (But Ferdinand de Lesseps, the French consul, listened and took notes.) The pasha rejected the canal but gladly accepted the newcomers' technical aid in constructing a dam across the Nile, just below Cairo. With Enfantin as director, a corps of Saint-Simonian polytechnicians sent out from France labored on the dam, apparently with competence, until work was interrupted by a raging plague.

Enfantin seems then to have been sobered, disillusioned, a prey to self-doubt. "I am beginning to be a little less of a monster," he wrote to a lady friend. Wearing native dress, he spent a year in Upper Egypt awaiting a revelation, visiting the antiquities, shooting crocodiles, and conducting intimate anthropological investigations among the native women.

He returned to France early in 1837, after three years' absence, to find his reform movement in ruins and the Ménilmontant estate foreclosed. He was now forty years old, unemployed, and in most men's eyes unemployable. He sought a government post, suggesting that of Minister of Commerce and Public Works. Persuaded that reform is best begun at the top rather than with the lowly, he invented the "royal apostolate." He would first convert the emperor of Austria, a priestly ruler, and then work down. But somehow he could never establish contact. He succeeded finally in joining a scientific mission to Algeria, but he lost the post because his report failed to deal with the subjects assigned him.

Thus at the end of the 1830's he relapsed into obscurity. Apparently he was running some sort of an express or forwarding service in Lyon. Such would be the normal end of the illuminate, the fantast, the aging outcast god. We imagine him conducting a little, perilous business, living in a dusty attic, clutching at chance acquaintances to tell his unsought tales. He would seem to have come to a destined outcome—failure. But on the contrary the defeated demigod found a resurrection among his human brothers.

It happened that Lyon was a center of railroad building. The early railroads of France were local lines, joining city to nearby city. Enfantin, whose conceptions were seldom less than cosmic, imagined a great trunk line from Le Havre to Marseilles joining sea to sea, cooperating with a Suez Canal, and challenging England's control of transport to the East. His proposals gained him public notice; he found himself the representative of the *Lyonnais* with the great bankers of Paris. He worked hand in hand with the Rothschilds, Pereires, Laffittes, Hottingers. They were dreamers, too; they welcomed his bold ideas. He was the chief promoter of the Paris-Lyon-Méditerranée line. In 1845 he became a director and in 1856 *administrateur*, or general manager.

Desirous of finding consistency in human behavior, we look for the fatal flaw, for the pathetic absurdity that would reveal itself in Enfantin's conduct and topple him into foredestined failure. He disappoints us. In business hours, at least, he was totally the businessman, prudent and competent. But he never disavowed the Saint-Simonian faith. He made the management and labor relationships of the P.-L.-M. a model for their time, with workers' mutual-aid funds, schools, libraries, and a museum. He proposed a *crédit intellectuel*, a central fund of knowledge, an intellectual bank, which should make loans of knowledge for production and provide subsidies for young men "who need six thousand francs before they can earn a sou."

He died, rich and full of honors, in 1864.

Evidently an ex-demigod can succeed in business. But at a cost. Monsieur l'Administrateur Enfantin had lost the divinity of Le Père Enfantin. And he never found the Female Messiah.

Cinque, whose mutiny became a cause célèbre, *in a portrait done by Nathaniel Jocelyn*

16 Cinque,
the Noble Mutineer

In the New Haven Colony Historical Society hangs a fine *Portrait of Cinque* by Nathaniel Jocelyn. The canvas shows a handsome young Negro with an African landscape at his back. The firm mouth, the suspicious eyes, suggest his hostility to the white world.

In the 1840's the name of Cinque was known to every newspaper reader in this country. He had led an uprising on a slave ship and murdered the white captain. In his ingenuous attempt to sail the vessel from Cuba to Africa, he arrived off the port of New York. Heading once more for Africa, he was fouled by the law off Montauk. His case, and that of his companions, became a sacred cause for the abolitionists. By the time they reached the Supreme Court, they had roused such ill feeling that they must be counted one of the series of events leading up to the Civil War.

In the end, Cinque and his mutineers sailed from New York for Africa amid the huzzas of our high-minded citizens.

On the west coast of Africa, seven degrees north of the equator, swelters the republic of Sierra Leone. In its hinterland live the Mendi people, a fine, sturdy race—"likely Negroes," as they used to be termed. Here was born, about 1813, Cinque (written *Sing-Gbe* by linguistic sticklers). He was the son of a petty chief. He married and had three children. His son he named God (*Gewaw* in Mendi). Perhaps there is here a hint of pride.

One day in the spring of 1839 he was walking in the bush when four men sprang out and seized him, bound his right hand to his neck, and added him to their troop of slaves. He was sold and resold until he found himself in the hold of a Portuguese slaver, the *Teçora*.

The slave dealers strove for economy in packing, to the point of being over-optimistic. The slave decks of the *Teçora* had only four feet of headroom. The slaves were chained in pairs, leg to leg, and stowed between decks in a sitting position. Each slave's knees embraced the back of the man in front. They were well fed with rice—in fact, forcibly overfed and so fattened for the market—but they had very little to drink. Here they remained for a voyage of three moons. Many men, women, and children died and had to be unchained and thrown over the side.

The *Teçora* landed Cinque and the rest of its cargo at a village near Havana. This was a violation of Spanish law. The importation of slaves into Spanish dominions was forbidden by Spain in 1820 in return for a payment of £450,000 by the British government. One would call this a very creditable humanitarian act of Great Britain, though no doubt someone will spring up to prove that the English were prompted by some commercial deviltry. In Cuba, the chief effect of the law was to raise the cost of the slave trade; officials had to be paid to wink at infractions of the law. The Cuban authorities had winked themselves into a state of chronic ophthalmia.

Dealers from Havana inspected the newly arrived Negroes, testing, exploring, estimating their bodies. Unfortunately for them, they did not examine Cinque's spirit. Don José Ruiz, known to the blacks as Pipi, a prosperous Cuban who had been educated in Connecticut, bought forty-nine men for $450 apiece, and Don Pedro Montez took three young girls, aged eight to thirteen. Cinque was one of the forty-nine men.

The two Spanish gentlemen designed to take their purchases to the Cuban port of Guanaja, three hundred miles east. To this end, they chartered "a long, low, black schooner," Baltimore-built, of about 120 tons burden, Captain Ferrer in command. Her pretty name was the *Amistad*, meaning "Friendship."

The *Amistad* set sail on June 28, 1839. Many of the slaves were unshackled now that they had officially entered slavery. The cook, a Cuban mulatto, was, it seems, a joker. When the captives inquired by signs where they were going, he gave them to understand that they were all to be killed and eaten. The news, said one of the slaves later, "made our hearts burn." There was plotting in the dark hold. Cinque, the most vigorous, intelligent, and determined of the party, naturally assumed command.

On the fourth night out, all the crew were asleep except the sailor at the helm. The captain and his personal slave, Antonio, were sleeping on mattresses on deck. They were suddenly awakened by a noise in the forecastle. Cinque and his men had surprised the sailors and seized some cane knives, murderous weapons with a two-foot blade. The mutineers ran aft, clattering and shouting. The captain, half asleep, thought the slaves must be hungry. "Go below and get some bread, and throw it to the niggers!" he shouted to Antonio. It was not bread the Negroes wanted but blood. Cinque struck the captain across the face and throat two or three times, killing him. Next, the knives accounted for the mulatto cook. Don Pedro Montez was slashed on the arm. He ran below, wrapped himself in a sail, and hid between two sugar barrels. A mutineer found him and rushed upon him, but was restrained by another Negro. Montez was taken on deck, faint with loss of blood, and was tied to Ruiz, wrist to wrist. The bodies of the captain and the cook were thrown overboard and the deck was washed down. Next day the sailors were put ashore in a small boat.

The reason Montez and Ruiz had been spared now became clear. Cinque informed his captives by signs that they were to sail the schooner back to Africa, back to the land of the Mendis. Montez had been a sailor, but he quailed at the thought of crossing the Atlantic in a ship provisioned for a short coastal journey and manned by a crew that could not fulfill his orders had they understood them. And if he should ever bring the ship successfully to its goal, he reasoned, his pay would probably be death.

The cruise that followed must still be unique in the history of the sea. The white men spelled each other at the wheel, and Captain Cinque, wearing as insigne a snuffbox tied to a string round his neck, watched the helmsmen closely. Once he ordered Montez to drop anchor on the high seas, to that sailor's horror. When the sun was visible, Cinque, with homing instinct, saw to it that the *Amistad* headed southeast. But Cinque could not read the compass. At night and on dark days, Montez brought the ship gently around to the north or west and used all his ingenuity to find a rescuing vessel or a kindly shore. He spoke several ships but was too well guarded to reveal his plight. An American schooner came alongside; the white men were sent below and the blacks bargained for supplies. The Americans sold them a demijohn of water for a gold doubloon, worth five dollars. The Americans sailed away; how could they suspect the rich?

The Negroes broke open and pillaged the cargo of the *Amistad*. They found supplies of wine and raisins and a great quantity of liquid medicines. They ate and drank everything indiscriminately, and ten of their number died. Cinque then established a rationing system and forbade his men to eat anything not given by his own hands.

Following an amazing course, the *Amistad* at length sighted land. It was the twentieth of August. A small vessel hove along-side and the white men again were sent below. One of the Negroes, Banna, had learned a few English words in Sierra Leone. "Africa? Mendiland?" he inquired. But the visitor would only reply, "We are New York Pilot Boat Number Three!"

The New Yorkers could make nothing of the mysterious craft and could see no likelihood of getting a fee for piloting. They gave the Negroes some apples and sailed away. The *Amistad* came about and again headed more or less in the direction of Africa.

The ship was badly in need of water for its journey. She coasted for four days eastward along the southern shore of Long Island, looking for a fair anchorage. Captain Cinque told the helmsman to steer for a light on Montauk Point, regarding it as a haven, but the tide bore the foul ship westward along the north shore of the peninsula to Culloden Point, just north of the village at Montauk. There the ship anchored and a party went ashore. Some wore only a handkerchief as a breechclout; others had blankets over their shoulders. They needed supplies, so they went to some houses and held up Spanish gold. They bought two dogs, for a doubloon apiece, and water and food. With these, they returned to the ship.

The next day they came again to shore, to cook their food on the beach. A daring party, headed by Captain Henry Green of Sag Harbor, paid them a visit, arriving in wagons. "Have you rum?" were Banna's first words. What they had, in fact, was gin; they sold the Negroes a bottle for a good price. Cinque told Banna to ask if there were slaves in this country. "No. This is a free country." "Are there any Spaniards here?" "No." At the answer, Cinque whistled and all the followers sprang up with African shouts of joy. The white men, frightened, turned to run for their guns, which they had left in their wagons. But the blacks held out their own guns as a sign of peace. They asked Captain Green to come on board and sail them to Sierra Leone.

He replied that he would think it over, and made a hastily courteous farewell. The Negroes returned to their ship.

As it happened, a coast survey brig, the *Washington*, Lieutenant Gedney in command, was in that part of the Sound. Lieutenant Gedney sighted the *Amistad*, and his seaman's eye saw something vaguely wrong with the long, low, black schooner. He sent a boat's crew over to her. When the boarding officer found only Negroes armed with cane knives on deck, he climbed into the rigging and, with pistol drawn, ordered them below. Cinque, with three hundred doubloons in his belt and the two dogs in his arms, sprang overboard. Underwater, he released the dogs, disengaged the belt, and emerged, it is said, a hundred yards away. A boat put out after him. He dived and dodged for forty minutes before he was taken. When he was brought back to the *Amistad*, he made what seemed to be an incendiary speech, exciting the Negroes. As a precaution, he was transferred to the *Washington* and put in irons.

The *Washington* convoyed her prize to New London and turned her over to the United States marshal. Montez and Ruiz were released.

A New London reporter thus described a visit to the schooner: "José Ruiz is the most striking instance of complacency and unalloyed delight we have ever witnessed, and it is not strange, since only yesterday his sentence was pronounced by the chief of the bucaniers, and his death song chanted by the grim crew, who gathered with uplifted sabres around his devoted head, which, as well as his arms, bears the scars of several wounds inflicted at the time of the murder of the ill-fated captain and crew. He sat smoking his Havana on deck, and to judge from the marytr-like serenity of his countenance, his emotions are such as rarely stir the heart of man. When Mr. Porter, the prize master, assured him of his safety, he threw his arms around his neck, while gushing tears coursing down his furrowed cheeks bespoke the overflowing transport of his soul.

Every now and then he clasped his hands, and with uplifted eyes, gave thanks to 'the Holy Virgin' who had led him out of his troubles. . . .

"On board the brig we also saw Cinque, the master spirit of this bloody tragedy, in irons. He is about five feet eight inches in height, 25 or 26 years of age, of erect figure, well built and very active. He is said to be a match for any two men on board the schooner. His countenance, for a native African, is unusually intelligent, evincing uncommon decision and coolness, with a composure characteristic of true courage, and nothing to mark him as a malicious man.

"By physiognomy and phrenology, he has considerable claim to benevolence. According to Gall and Spurzheim [authors of a system of phrenology] his moral sentiments and intellectual faculties predominate considerably over his animal propensities. He is said, however, to have killed the Captain and crew with his own hand, by cutting their throats. He has also several times attempted the life of Señor Montez, and the backs of several poor negroes are scored with scars of blows inflicted by his lash to keep them in subjection. He expects to be executed, but nevertheless manifests a *sang froid* worthy of a stoic under similar circumstances."

The Negroes, when examined later, blamed their scars on the lash of the white masters on the voyage from Africa and said that vinegar and gunpowder had been rubbed in their wounds. But this New London reporter was after what would now be called a colorful story.

"With Captain Gedney, the surgeon of the port, and others," he wrote, "we visited the schooner, and there we saw such a sight as we never saw before and never wish to see again. The bottom and sides of this vessel are covered with barnacles and sea grass, while her rigging and sails presented an appearance worthy of the Flying Dutchman, after her fabled cruise. . . . On her deck were grouped amid various foods and arms the remnant of her Ethiop crew, some decked in the most fantastic manner, in silks and finery pilfered from the cargo, while others, in a state of nudity, emaciated to mere skeletons, lay coiled upon the decks. Here could be seen a negro with white pantaloons, and the sable shirt which nature gave him, and a planter's broad-brimmed hat upon his head with a string of gewgaws about his neck; and another with a linen cambric shirt, whose bosom was worked by some dark-eyed daughter of Spain, while his nether proportions were enveloped in a shawl of gauze or Canton crepe. Around the windlass were gathered the three little girls, from eight to thirteen years of age, the very image of health and gladness. . . .

"On the forward hatch we unconsciously rested our hand on a cold object, which we soon discovered to be a naked corpse, enveloped in a pall of black bombazine. On removing its folds, we beheld the rigid countenance and glazed eye of a poor negro who died last night. His mouth was unclosed and still wore the ghastly expression of his last struggle. Near him, like some watching fiend, sat the most horrible creature we ever saw in human shape, an object of terror to the very blacks, who said he was a cannibal. His teeth projected at almost right angles from his mouth, while his eyes had a most savage and demoniac expression.

"We were glad to leave this vessel, as the exhalations from her hold and deck were like anything but 'gales wafted over the gardens of Gul.' "

The reporter did an injustice to the "watching fiend," who was no cannibal but a dandy from the Konno country, with his incisor teeth pressed outward and filed and a diamond-shaped tattoo mark on the forehead. When, at the trial, he was asked the reason for his dental display, he explained it was "to make the ladies love him."

The Negroes were jailed, charged with murder and piracy. Lieutenant Gedney brought a suit in admiralty, claiming salvage for himself, and hence possession of the schooner and its contents. The Spanish minister presented to the United States Department of State a claim for the ship, slaves, and cargo, on behalf of the king of Spain. But the enemies of slavery were busy too. Here, on the soil of a free state, were a group of men who had been kidnapped from their African homes and had killed only to gain a freedom to which they were entitled, even by Spanish law.

A committee of abolitionists was formed to defend the prisoners. Its first difficulty was that of communication. Banna's English was too scanty to be of much service. The ingenious Professor J. W. Gibbs of the Yale Divinity School solved the problem. He obtained from the captives their words for the numerals from one to ten. He then went to the New York docks, and wherever he found a Negro sailor he accosted him by counting up to ten in Mendi. After frightening a good many blacks, he had the thrilling experience of finding a colored sailor who laughed with delight. This was a Mendi youth who had been part of the cargo of a Portuguese slaver captured by the English. He had learned English in Sierra Leone and had enlisted as a sailor on Her Majesty's brig of war *Buzzard*. The *Buzzard* (who names the British naval vessels, anyway?) was lying in New York harbor. The captain of the *Buzzard* graciously lent the interpreter, Kaw-we-li, whose name had been strangely anglicized as James Covey, to the *Amistad* committee. And now the story of the captives came fully to light, stirring the emotions of most Americans north of Mason and Dixon's line.

At the hearing of the salvage case, in Hartford, Ruiz and Montez appeared and claimed possession of the slaves. An indictment for piracy and murder was brought against Cinque and his men by a grand jury. However, the judge instructed the grand jury to rule that the Negroes had committed no crime against the laws of the United States but that the question whether they were slave or free must be decided by the courts.

The prisoners, numbering thirty-nine men and three girls, now lodged in the New Haven jail, were given a certain amount of freedom. They were exercised daily on the Green, Cinque leading them in remarkable feats of agility. The somersaults of his lieutenant, Grabeau, were particularly applauded. The jailer charged an entrance fee of a shilling for visitors to his jail.

The case of the *Amistad* captives grew steadily in importance. The government of Spain angrily demanded their extradition. Great Britain made a plea for leniency. The case begat other, smaller cases, actions, and suits, such as an action by the abolitionists, in the name of Cinque, against Ruiz and Montez for damages for false imprisonment. President Martin Van Buren, worried about the Southern vote in the 1840 elections, sent a warship to New Haven with orders to seize the Negroes immediately if the trial should go against them, before the abolitionists could have time to file an appeal. But the court ruled that the Negroes were kidnapped into slavery and hence legally free. An appeal was taken by the government.

Meanwhile the captives had been transferred to the jail in Westville (a little beyond where the Yale Bowl now stands). Charitable people taught them English and even reading and writing, with special attention to their moral and religious instruction. They learned some of the catechism and four or five hymns. The abolitionist newspapers reported delightedly on their progress. A show of wax figures of the captives toured the country. Nathaniel Jocelyn, New Haven painter and abolitionist, painted the fine portrait. The New York press, which had at first been hostile and fearful, turned kindly. The *Sun* thus described Cinque: "His eye can exhibit every variety of thought, from the cool contempt of a haughty chieftain to the high resolve which would be sustained through martyrdom. . . . His nostrils he can contract or dilate at pleasure. . . . Many white men might take a lesson in dignity and forbearance from the African chieftain."

Finally the case came before the United States Supreme Court, in February, 1841. Ex-President John Quincy Adams eloquently argued the case for the captives. The Supreme Court ruled that the Negroes were not slaves or subjects of Spain. They must "be declared free, and be dismissed from the custody of the Court, and go without delay."

The *Amistad* had already been sold with her cargo for the benefit of the original owners and to pay the salvage claims.

When the news of their release was brought to the prisoners, they were incoherent with joy. Led by one of their teachers, they sang their favorite hymn (to the tune of "Auld Lang Syne"):

> When I can read my title clear
> To mansions in the skies,
> I'll bid farewell to every fear,
> And wipe my weeping eyes.

Only Cinque the wise remained pensive. When the newspaper report was read to him, he observed, "Paper lie sometimes."

Through the efforts of the *Amistad* committee, the Negroes were taken to Farmington, near Hartford, and lodged with abolitionist farmers during the summer while the committee raised funds to send them back to Africa. None of them wished to remain in America; the cold weather, it appears, made New England life unendurable for them. Letters, allegedly by the victims, were published in the abolitionist newspapers to help along the campaign. The letters are pious and naïve, full of comically winning turns of phrase in what certainly sounds like a Negro stage dialect.

In the autumn, the Negroes were taken on a barnstorming tour from Boston to Philadelphia to help raise money for their return journey. It was a great success. "We would go farther to see Cinque than Napoleon Bonaparte!" vowed the reporter for the Lynn *Record*. He also noted that twenty-five dollars was contributed to the repatriation fund by a Cambridge lady who sold pies, custards, etc., near the colleges, "and whom Professor Hedge, in familiar conversation, humorously denominated 'a very *pious* woman'!"

At New York's Broadway Tabernacle, which stood between Worth Street and Catherine Lane, the Negroes delighted a capacity audience with their exercises in spelling, reading from the Bible, and hymn singing. "They also sang a native song with an energy of manner, a wildness of music, and at times a sweetness of melody, which were altogether peculiar," remarked the *Journal of Commerce*. Cinque addressed the audience in Mendi with great power and effect. He was described as "a true specimen of the eloquence of nature." Lewis Tappan, the great New York abolitionist, said of him: "He was pronounced a powerful natural orator, and one born to sway the minds of his fellow men. Should he be converted and become a preacher of the cross in Africa what delightful results may be anticipated!"

Tappan's hope might have been dampened by a remark of Cinque's. One of Cinque's companions, speaking of the murder of the captain and the cook of the *Amistad*, said that if it were to be done over, he would pray for them instead of killing them. Cinque smiled and shook his head. "Yes," he said, "I would pray for 'em—and kill 'em too."

Cinque and his band at last set sail from New York in the brig *Gentlemen*, chartered for their journey, on December 2, 1841. They were accompanied by five missionaries. News of their safe arrival in Sierra Leone reached America in mid-March.

Africa took its revenge upon the West. In the mission which was established by the five pioneers, at least twenty missionaries died in thirty years. Most of the Negroes relapsed gently into their old ways. Even Cinque reverted to what is known as savagery.

The homing impulse in his heart had brought him back at last to his own hut in the jungle. To find his way there, he had committed murder, had captained a ship, and had become a symbol and a celebrity and a breeder of discord. The poetic ending of his story would have been a total return to his tribal life and a total forgetting of the strange nation which had at the same time imprisoned him and exalted him.

But in fact he seems to have been bored by tribal life in Mendiland. He was used now to white men and their little luxuries. He returned finally to the mission station and served there as interpreter. He died in about 1880.

The perfectionist paradise at Oneida, New York, on a peaceful day in the last century

17 Mr. Noyes,
the Oneida Community,
and Stirpiculture

Sin, the conviction of sin, the assurance of punishment for sin, pervaded pioneer America like the fever and ague, and took nearly as many victims. Taught that in Adam's fall we had sinnèd all, threatened with hell-fire by revivalist preachers, tortured by the guilt of intimate offenses, earnest youths whipped themselves into madness and suicide, and died crying that they had committed the sin against the Holy Ghost, which is unforgivable, though no one knows quite what it is.

The year 1831 was known as the Great Revival, when itinerant evangelists powerfully shook the bush and gathered in a great harvest of sinners. In September of that year John Humphrey Noyes, a twenty-year-old Dartmouth graduate and a law student in Putney, Vermont, attended such a revival. He was in a mood of metaphysical despair, aggravated by a severe cold. During the exhortings the conviction of salvation came to him. Light gleamed upon his soul, attaining meridian splendor. "Ere the day was done," he wrote later, "I had concluded to devote myself to the service and ministry of God."

Noyes was a young man of good family. His father was a Dartmouth graduate, a successful merchant in Putney, and a congressman. John was a bookish youth, delighting in history, romance, and poetry of a martial character, such as the lives of Napoleon or of the Crusaders or Sir Walter Scott's *Marmion*. He was red-haired and freckled, and thought himself too homely ever to consider marriage. But when he began preaching his face shone like an angel's; one of his sons later averred that "there was about him an unmistakable and somewhat unexpected air of spiritual assurance." According to his phrenological analysis, his bumps of amativeness, combativeness, and self-esteem were large, his benevolence and philoprogenitiveness very large. His life confirmed these findings.

After his mystical experience in Putney, Noyes spent a year in the Andover Theological Seminary (Congregational). He found his teachers and companions lukewarm in piety, and devoted himself to an intensive study of the New Testament, most of which he could recite by heart. A divine direction—"I know that ye seek Jesus which was crucified. He is not here" —sent him from Andover to the Yale Theological Seminary in New Haven. There he came in contact with the doctrine of perfectionism and was allured by it.

Perfectionism asserted that men may be freed from sin and attain in this life the perfect holiness necessary to salvation. It rejected therefore the consequences of original sin and went counter to the Calvinistic dogma of total depravity. Perfectionism took shape early in the nineteenth century and found lodgment among adventurous groups in New Haven, Newark, and Albany and in villages of central New York, "the burned-over district," where religion smote with a searing flame. Perfectionism was likely to develop into antinomianism, the contention that faith frees the faithful from the claims and obligations of Old Testament moral law. And antinomianism led readily to scandal, as when three perfectionist missionaries, two men and a sister of one of them, were tarred and feathered for sleeping together in one bed.

Though suspected of perfectionist heresy, Noyes was licensed to preach in August, 1833. At about the same time, he made a sensational discovery: Jesus Christ had announced that He would return during the lifetime of some of His disciples. Jesus could not be mistaken; therefore the Second Coming of Christ had taken place in A.D. 70. The "Jewish cycle" of religious history then ended and a "Gentile cycle" began, in which the Church has improperly usurped the authority of the apostles. We live no longer in an age of prophecy and promise, but in an age of fulfillment. Perfect holiness is attainable in this life, as well as guaranteed deliverance from sin.

Noyes found this revelation by fasting, prayer, and diligent search of the Scriptures. At divine command he announced it in a sermon to the Free Church of New Haven on February 20, 1834. "I went home with a feeling that I had committed myself irreversibly, and on my bed that night I received the baptism which I desired and expected. Three times in quick succession a stream of eternal love gushed through my heart, and rolled back again to its source. 'Joy unspeakable and full of glory' filled my soul. All fear and doubt and condemnation passed away. I knew that my heart was clean, and that the Father and the Son had come and made it their abode."

This was all very well, but next day the word ran through New Haven, "Noyes says he is perfect!" with the inevitable corollary, "Noyes is crazy!" The authorities promptly expelled him from the seminary and revoked his license to preach. But the perfect are proof against imperfect human detractors. "I have taken away their license to sin, and they keep on sinning," said Noyes. "So, though they have taken away my license to preach, I shall keep on preaching." This he did, with some success. His first convert was Miss Abigail Merwin of Orange, Connecticut, with whom he felt himself sealed in the faith.

Nevertheless his way was far from smooth. He had yet to pass through what he called "the dark valley of conviction."

He went to New York and wandered the streets in a kind of frenzy, catching a little sleep by lying down in a doorway, or on the steps of City Hall, or on a bench at the Battery. He sought the most ill-famed regions of the city. "I descended into cellars where abandoned men and women were gathered, and talked familiarly with them about their ways of life, beseeching them to believe on Christ, that they might be saved from their sins. They listened to me without abuse." Tempted by the Evil One, he doubted all, even the Bible, even Christ, even Abigail Merwin, whom he suspected to be Satan in angelic disguise. But after drinking the dregs of the cup of trembling he emerged purified and secure. He retreated to Putney for peace and shelter. His friends, even his sister, thought him deranged. But such was the power of his spirit that he gathered a little group of adepts, relatives, and friends, to accept his revelation.

Miss Abigail Merwin, however, took fright, married a schoolteacher, and removed to Ithaca, New York. Noyes followed her there—a rather ungentlemanly procedure. After a few months she left her husband, but not for Noyes's arms— only to return to her father in Connecticut.

Noyes was delighted with the pretty village of Ithaca, with his lodging in the Clinton House, and especially with the broad-minded printers, unafraid of publishing heresies and liberal with credit. On August 20, 1837, he established a periodical, the *Witness*, for a subscription rate of one dollar, or, if a dollar should be inconvenient, for nothing. The issue of September 23 reverberated far beyond the subscription list of faithful perfectionists. Noyes had written a private letter expressing his radical views on marriage among the perfect. By a violation of confidence, this had reached the free-thinking editor of a paper called *The Battle-Axe*. Noyes, disdaining evasion, acknowledged in the *Witness* his authorship of the letter and reiterated his startling conclusions. The essential of "the

Battle-Axe letter" lies in the concluding words: "When the will of God is done on earth as it is in heaven, *there will be no marriage*. The marriage supper of the Lamb is a feast at which *every dish is free to every guest*. Exclusiveness, jealousy, quarreling, have no place there, for the same reason as that which forbids the guests at a thanksgiving dinner to claim each his separate dish, and quarrel with the rest for his rights. In a holy community, there is no more reason why sexual intercourse should be restrained by law, than why eating and drinking should be—and there is as little occasion for shame in the one as in the other. . . . The guests of the marriage supper may each have his favorite dish, each a dish of his own procuring, and that without the jealousy of exclusiveness."

Ungallant as this statement is in its characterization of women as dishes to pass, it states a reasonable protest against the egotisms of marriage. One may readily perceive in it also a secret resentment against the unfaithful Abigail Merwin. One may even interpret it as the erotic outburst of repressed impulse. Noyes, an impassioned, amorous type, was still a virgin.

Noyes was soon vouchsafed a sign, almost a miracle. When he was eighty dollars in debt to an Ithaca printer, he received from a disciple in Vermont, Miss Harriet A. Holton of Westminster, a letter enclosing a gift of exactly eighty dollars. He paid his bill, returned to Putney, and after a decent interval, forgetting the perfectionist views of the *Battle-Axe* letter, proposed exclusive marriage to Miss Holton. The two were formally united in Chesterfield, New Hampshire, in June, 1838. For a honeymoon they drove to Albany to buy a second-hand printing press, with more of Harriet's money.

Thus began the Putney Community, which at first consisted only of John Noyes and his wife, several of his brothers and sisters, and a small cluster of converts from the neighborhood. They lived in a group, sharing possessions and duties. Their chief occupations were spiritual exercises in pursuit of holiness and the printing of the *Witness* on their own press. Noyes had no great liking for sheer honest toil for its own sake; he wished to secure for all the freedom for spiritual development. The women prepared one hot meal a day—breakfast. Thereafter the hungry had to help themselves in the kitchen.

Noyes was restless in the monotonous peace of Putney. His wife inherited $9,000 in 1844; Noyes was provoked to fantastic visions. He wrote his wife: "In order to subdue the world to Christ we must carry religion into money-making." He proposed first a theological seminary for perfectionism, then agencies in Boston and New York to distribute their spiritual goods. "Then we must advance into foreign commerce, and as our means enlarge we must cover the ocean with our ships and the whole world with the knowledge of God. This is a great scheme, but not too great for God. . . . Within ten years we will plant the standard of Christ on the highest battlements of the world."

Though allured by such shimmering visions, he had to deal with present problems. An urgent personal problem was that of sex. His wife was pregnant five times in six years. She endured long agonies ending in four stillbirths. The only surviving child was Theodore, born in 1841. John Noyes suffered with his wife, and he protested against cruel nature, perhaps against God. Surely women were not made to suffer so. Surely there was a better way. A perfectionist could not brook flagrant imperfection. Noyes's habit was to seek and find a better way, and then sanctify and capitalize it. The better way turned out to be male continence.

Noyes had been trained in the Puritan ethic, which did not regard marital sex as unholy. Nevertheless the consequences of male egotism horrified him. "It is as foolish and cruel to expend one's seed on a wife merely for the sake of getting rid of it," he wrote, "as it would be to fire a gun at one's best friend merely for the sake of unloading it." After his wife's disasters he lived for a time chaste by her side. But chastity proving to be no solution at all, he embraced male continence, of which the definition embarrasses the chaste pen. When embarrassed, the chaste pen may decently quote. One of the community disciples, H. J. Seymour, thus defined the practice: "checking the flow of amative passion before it reaches the point of exposing the man to the loss of virile energy, or the woman to the danger of undesired child-bearing." Or, with Latin decorum, *coitus reservatus;* or, more colloquially, everything but.

This was not actually the beginning of birth-control advocacy. In 1831 Robert Dale Owen, the reformer of New Harmony, Indiana, published his *Moral Physiology*, advocating *coitus interruptus*, which Noyes scored as substituting self-indulgence for self-control. A year later a Boston physician, Charles Knowlton, published *The Fruits of Philosophy; or the Private Companion of Young Married People*, pointing to the menace of excessive child-bearing and eventual overpopulation, and recommending contraception. Dr. Knowlton and his publisher were accused of blasphemy. Their case was carried to the Supreme Court, and the two men were condemned to spend several months in jail.

"Amativeness is to life as sunshine is to vegetation," wrote Noyes twelve years later in his *Bible Argument Defining the Relation of the Sexes in the Kingdom of Heaven*. "Ordinary sexual intercourse (in which the amative and propagative functions are confounded) is a momentary affair, terminating in exhaustion and disgust. . . . Adam and Eve . . . sunk the spiritual in the sensual in their intercourse with each other, by pushing prematurely beyond the amative to the propagative, and so became ashamed." In the future society, "as propagation will become a science, so amative intercourse will become one of the 'fine arts.' Indeed it will rank above music, painting, sculpture, &c.; for it combines the charms and the benefits of them all."

All this is very noble and high-minded; but we are trained to look for—and we usually find—a casuistical serpent in the gardens, who is able to transform impulses into ideals, even into new theologies. The serpent in this case was Mary Cragin, who with her husband, George, had joined the Putney Community. Mary Cragin was a charmer, and, to put it badly, sexy. (Do not condemn her; some are, some aren't. This is a well-known fact.) Noyes feared that she might "become a Magdalene" if he did not save her. One evening in the woods, John and Mary discovered that they were united by a deep spiritual bond. "We took some liberty of embracing, and Mrs. George distinctly gave me to understand that she was ready for the full consummation." But Noyes insisted on a committee meeting with the respective spouses. "We gave each other full liberty, and so entered into marriage in quartette form. The last part of the interview was as amiable and happy as a wedding, and a full consummation . . . followed."

This was Noyes's first infidelity, according to the world's idiom. He found a more grandiloquent term for it—complex marriage, to contrast with the restrictiveness of simple marriage. Heaven beamed on the participants. "Our love is of God; it is destitute of exclusiveness, each one rejoicing in the happiness of the others," said Mary. The Putney Community, in general, applauded; some, under direction, adopted the new cure for marital selfishness. It appears that some Puritan wives, as well as husbands, were secretly weary of the "scanty and monotonous fare" provided by monogamy.

But righteous Putney soon had hints of the goings-on and uprose in anger. On October 26, 1847, Noyes was arrested, charged with adultery, and released, pending trial, in $2,000 bail. Noyes declared himself guiltless, insisting that in common law no tort has been committed if no one is injured. "The head and front and whole of our offense is communism of love. . . . If this is the unpardonable sin in the world, we are sure it is the beauty and glory of heaven." But in fear of mob violence from "the barbarians of Putney" he thought it well to jump bail, following the counsel of the highest authority: "When they persecute you in this city, flee ye into another."

A refuge awaited the persecuted saints in the burned-over district of central New York, a region familiar to Noyes. A group of perfectionists offered the Putneyans a sawmill and forty acres of woodland on Oneida Creek, halfway between Syracuse and Utica. It was a bland, fertile, welcoming country, suitable for an Eden. By good omen, the spot was the exact geographical center of New York State, if one overlooked Long Island.

In mid-February, 1848, "the year of the great change," the pilgrims began to arrive. Defying the upstate winter, lodging in abandoned Indian cabins, they set to with a will to build a community dwelling and workshops. Some of the neighbors looked at them askance; most welcomed these honest, pious, industrious newcomers, and some even were converted to perfectionism and threw in their lot with the colony.

The early years were the heroic age of Oneida. All worked together, cutting and sawing timber, digging clay and baking bricks, building simple houses, clearing land for vegetable gardens. Everyone took his or her turn at the household tasks. All work was held in equal honor, without prestige connotations. Noyes recognized that most American experiments in communal life had foundered because they were established on the narrow base of agriculture; his communism would live on industry. Thus Oneida marketed canned fruits and vegetables, sewing silk, straw hats, mop sticks, traveling bags, and finally silver tableware. Its traps for animals, from rodents to bears, became famous as far as Alaska and Siberia. The cruelty of traps seldom occurred to the makers, who were frontiersmen as well as perfectionists. Sympathy with suffering beasts and the conservation of wildlife were concepts still undeveloped.

To a critic, Noyes replied that since God had covered the earth with vermin, Oneida simply helped to cleanse it. Salesmen, known only as peddlers, were sent out to market the wares. On their return, they were given a Turkish bath and a sharp examination on faith and practice, a spiritual rubdown to expunge the stains of the unregenerate world.

The Oneida Community prospered. The numbers of the faithful rose. The great Mansion House, the community home, was begun in 1860 and completed a dozen years later. It is a far-wandering red-brick building or group of buildings, standing on a knoll amid magnificent fat trees. Harmoniously proportioned, with its towers, mansard roofs, and tall French windows, it is a superb example of mid-nineteenth-century architecture. Its message is security, peace, and material comfort. The interior is graced with fine woodwork and decorations. The parlors, the excellent library, the lovely assembly hall, are redolent with memories, jealously preserved and proudly recounted. Here live a number of descendants of the original Oneidans, together with some lodgers, still regarded with kindly pity as "foreign bodies."

The memories, second-hand though they are, are all of a happy time, of a golden age long lost. John Humphrey Noyes, affectionately referred to by his grandchildren as "the Honorable John," was a cheerful person, and imposed happiness on his great family. The story is told of a visitor who asked her guide: "What is the fragrance I smell here in this house?" The guide answered: "It may be the odor of crushed selfishness." There was no money within the Oneida economy, no private possession, no competition for food and shelter, no exclusiveness, and hence little rivalry.

All worked and played together. Whenever possible, work was done on the "bee" system; thus a party of men and women would make handbags on the lawn, while a dramatic voice read a novel aloud. Classes were conducted in such recondite subjects as Greek and Hebrew. Dances, and respectable card games like euchre and whist, were in favor. Amateur theatricals were a constant diversion. The productions of *The Merchant of Venice*, *The Merry Wives of Windsor*, and especially of *H. M. S. Pinafore* were famous as far as Utica and Syracuse. Music was encouraged, with an orchestra and much vocalization. Music, Noyes mused, was closely related to sexual love; it was an echo of the passions. However, music harbored a menace; it gave rise to rivalries, jealousies, and vanities, to what Noyes reproved as "prima donna fever."

Noyes had strong views on dress. He called the contrast of men's and women's costumes immodest in that it proclaimed the distinction of sex. "In a state of nature, the difference between a man and a woman could hardly be distinguished at a distance of five hundred yards, but as men and women dress, their sex is telegraphed as far as they can be seen. Women's dress is a standing lie. It proclaims that she is not a two-legged animal, but something like a churn, standing on castors. . . . Gowns operate as shackles, and they are put on that sex which has most talent in the legs."

From the beginning at Oneida a new dress for women was devised, loose skirts to the knee with pantalets below, thus approximating a gentleman's frock coat and trousers. Some visitors were shocked, some were amused; few were allured. Indeed, the specimens remaining in the community's collections and the representations in photographs hardly seem beautiful. But the wearers rejoiced in their new freedom of movement. They cut their hair, in despite of St. Paul. It is asserted that they both looked and felt younger.

For thirty years the community, a placid island amid the stormy seas of society, lived its insulated life. It numbered, at its peak, three hundred members. It was undisturbed, except by invasions of visitors, brought on bargain excursions by the railroads. As many as a thousand appeared on a single day, picnicking on the grounds, invading the workshops and private quarters. They were welcomed; but on their departure all the Oneidans turned to in order to collect the scatterings, to scrub out the tobacco stains on the parquet floors.

The structure, the doctrine, the persistence of Oneida made a unique social phenomenon. It was consciously a family, with Noyes as father. As Constance Noyes Robertson says, it substituted "for the small unit of home and family and individual possessions the larger unit of group-family and group-family life." Its faith was "Bible Communism." Though it held aloof from all churches and deconsecrated the Sabbath, it was pietistic, in demanding the regeneration of society by rejecting competition, a money economy, and private ownership, whether of goods or persons. But it was not Marxian, for it made no mention of class warfare, of a revolution to come, of proletarian dictatorship.

The internal organization of the community was loose and vague, depending largely on the will of Noyes. Justice and discipline were administered informally, if at all. To provide correction, Noyes trusted chiefly to a procedure known as mutual criticism. Saint Paul had said: "Speak every man truth with his neighbor; for we are members one of another"; and the Apostle James: "Confess your faults one to another." When an individual offered himself for criticism, or was designated from above, a committee prepared his "trial," but any member might join in the proceedings. Noyes insisted that the trial be conducted with love, respect, and sincerity. The subject was informed of his secret faults, of shortcomings he had not suspected. He learned that his very virtues, on which he had flattered himself, were only disguised vices. There are strong hints that, as in all conventional societies, the critics derived pleasure from revealing home truths to imperfect fellow-members. A transcript of the proceedings was posted and often printed. The subject of this primitive psychoanalysis was likely to suffer dreadfully from his new self-knowledge. "I was shaken from center to circumference," said one. "I was metaphorically stood upon my head and allowed to drain until all the self-righteousness had dripped out of me." Afterwards the subject felt enlightened, purified, happy. "Mutual criticism," said Noyes, "subordinates the I-spirit to the We-spirit."

It also made the subjects, mostly brooding introspectives, for a time the center of interest and concern for the whole community. Mutual criticism, under the name of "krinopathy," was even used as a therapeutic device to cure children's colds, with, it was said, remarkable success.

Of the various Oneida institutions, the most fascinating to the prurient observer is the organization of sex behavior. Since the community was a single great family, there could be within it no marrying and giving in marriage. Each was married to all, Noyes insisted; every man was husband and brother to every woman. Love, far from being a sin, was holy, a sacrament; in the sexual experience one escaped from egotism and selfhood into the ecstasy of communion. Every effort must be to "abound"—one of Noyes's favorite words. One must spend, not hoard. The human heart seldom realizes its possibilities; it "is capable of loving any number of times and any number of persons; the more it loves the more it can love." One had only to look at surrounding society to recognize the evils of exclusive marriage, the chains binding unmatched natures, the secret adulteries, actual or of the heart, the hate-filled divorces, women's diseases, prostitution, masturbation, licentiousness in general.

Noyes maintained that sexual love was not naturally restricted to pairs, that second marriages were often the happiest. "Men and women find universally (however the fact may be concealed) that their susceptibility to love is not burned out by one honeymoon, or satisfied by one lover." The body should assert its rights; religion should make use of the senses as helpers of devotion. Sexual shame, the consequence of the fall of man, is factitious and irrational. "Shame ought to be banished from the company of virtue, though in the world it has stolen the very name of virtue. . . . Shame gives rise to the theory that sexual offices have no place in heaven. Anyone who has true modesty would sooner banish singing from heaven than sexual music." Beware, said Noyes, of one who proclaims that he is free from sexual desire, beware of religious teachers with fondling hands. Beware especially of Dr. Josiah Gridley of Southampton, Massachusetts, who boasts that he could carry a virgin in each hand without the least stir of passion. In short, "you must not serve the lusts of the flesh; if you do you will be damned. You must not make monks of yourself; if you do you will be damned. You must find a way to make your senses promote your spirituality, or you will be damned."

One might suspect that these doctrines would have led to outright antinomianism and to general orgies. Nothing of the sort occurred, thanks to the watchful care of Noyes and thanks to the character of the Oneidans, devout and rather humorless seekers for perfection. The system of complex marriage, or pantagamy, begun in Putney, was instituted. A man might request the privilege of a private visit with a lady, or a lady might take the initiative, for "in all nature the female element invites and the male responds." The request was submitted to a committee of elders, headed by Noyes, who gave the final approval or disapproval. The mate besought had the right of refusal. It was recommended that older women should initiate young men, and vice versa. Thus the young men were expertly guided in the practice of male continence, while the maturer men undertook without complaint the education of the maidens. The committee was also concerned to break up "exclusive and idolatrous attachments" of two persons of the same age for each other, for these bred selfishness. We are assured that complex marriage worked admirably, that for many life became a continuous courtship. "Amativeness, the lion of the tribe of human passions, is conquered and civilized among us." But the records are unwontedly reticent on the details of the system's operation. Only one scandal is remembered, when an unworthy recruit tried to force his attentions on the women, and was expelled through a window into a snowdrift. One suspects that in spite of all the spiritual training there were heartaches and hidden anger, and much whispering and giggling at the sound of midnight footsteps on the stairs.

The flaw in the system of continence was the threatening sterilization of the movement—the fate of the Shakers. Noyes recognized the danger, and in his *Bible Argument* of 1848 had proposed scientific propagation to replace random or involuntary propagation. But the time was not yet ripe. In the difficult early years of Oneida, Noyes discouraged childbearing, and his docile followers produced only forty-four offspring in twenty years. Then increasing prosperity permitted him to take steps for the perpetuation of his community. Early in 1869, he proposed the inauguration of stirpiculture, or the scientific improvement of the human stock by breeding. "Every race-horse, every straight-backed bull, every premium pig tells us what we can do and what we must do for men." Oneida should be a laboratory for the preparation of the great race of the future.

The Oneidans, especially the younger ones, greeted the proposal with enthusiasm. Fifty-three young women signed these resolutions:

"1. That we do not belong to ourselves in any respect, but that we do belong to *God*, and second to Mr. Noyes as God's true representative.

"2. That we have no rights or personal feelings in regard to childbearing which shall in the least degree oppose or embarrass him in his choice of scientific combinations.

"3. That we will put aside all envy, childishness and self-seeking, and rejoice with those who are chosen candidates; that we will, if necessary, become martyrs to science, and cheerfully resign all desire to become mothers, if for any reason Mr. Noyes deem us unfit material for propagation. Above all, we offer ourselves 'living sacrifices' to God and true Communism."

At the same time thirty-eight young men made a corresponding declaration to Noyes: "The undersigned desire you may feel that we most heartily sympathize with your purpose in regard to scientific propagation, and offer ourselves to be used in forming any combinations that may seem to you desirable. We claim no rights. We ask no privileges. We desire to be servants of the truth. With a prayer that the grace of God will help us in this resolution, we are your true soldiers."

Thus began the first organized experiment in human eugenics. For several years Noyes directed all the matings, on the basis of physical, spiritual, moral, and intellectual suitability. In 1875 a committee of six men and six women was formed to issue licenses to propagate. The selective process bore some bitter fruit. The eliminated males particularly were unhappy, unconsoled by the reflection that in animal breeding one superior stud may serve many females. Noyes relented in his scientific purpose so far as to permit one child to each male applicant. There was also some covert grumbling that Noyes, then in his sixties, elected himself to father nine children, by several mates. Eugenically, to be sure, he was entirely justified; there could be no doubt of his superiority.

The results of the stirpicultural experiment have not been scientifically studied, though an article by Hilda Herrick Noyes, prepared in 1921, gives some valuable statistical information. About one hundred men and women took part; eighty-one became parents, producing fifty-eight living children and four stillborn. No mothers were lost during the experiment;

no defective children were produced. The health of the off-spring was exceptionally good; their longevity has far surpassed the average expectations of life. The children, and the children's children, constitute a very superior group, handsome and intelligent. Many have brilliantly conducted the affairs of their great manufacturing corporation; others have distinguished themselves in public service, the arts, and literature.

The integration of the children into the community caused some difficulties. The mother kept her child until he was weaned and could walk; then he was transferred to the Children's House, though he might return to his mother for night care. Noyes, with his ideal of the community family, disapproved of egotistic, divisive "special love"; the mothers were permitted to see their children only once or twice a week. The children were excellently educated in the nursery school, the kindergarten, and the grammar school by teachers chosen for their competence and natural liking for the young. If the children cried for their mothers, they were severely reproved for "partiality" or "stickiness." One graduate of the Children's House remembered that when he was forbidden to visit his mother he went berserk. Another recalled her agony when she caught sight of her mother after a fortnight's enforced separation. The child begged her mother not to leave her—and the mother fled for fear of a penalty of an additional week's separation from her child.

The atmosphere of the Children's House was, in short, that of a friendly orphanage. If the disruption of the family units had any bad psychic effects on the children, they have not been recorded. Children accept their world as it is; they know no other. The memories of the Oneida boys and girls are mostly of happy schooldays under kind teachers, days of laughter, play, and delightful learning. The judgment of one eminent product, Pierrepont B. Noyes, is surely correct, that the community system was harder on the mothers than on the children.

The fathers were more remote from their children than were the mothers. Pierrepont Noyes admits: "Father never seemed a father to me in the ordinary sense." The system reflects indeed the character of John Humphrey Noyes. He was the Father of his people, the semidivine begetter of a community, and he loved the community communally. He saw no reason to encourage family bonds, "partiality," among the faithful, at cost to the community spirit. He seems to have shown little personal affection for his sons after the flesh. No doubt a phrenologist would have noted that his bump of parental love was small. One is tempted to go further, to see in his disregard for his children a certain horror of paternity, a deep-implanted remembrance of his four stillborn babies, of his wife's sufferings and his own.

The rumors of strange sex practices roused the righteous and the orthodox, already angered by Oneida's nonobservance of the Sabbath and rejection of church affiliations. A professor at Hamilton College, John W. Mears, still the bogeyman of Oneida after a hundred years, began in 1873 a long campaign to destroy the community and its band of sinners. Though most of the inhabitants and newspaper editors of the region defended Noyes and his followers, though local justice could find no grounds for prosecution, the churches demanded action against "the ethics of the barnyard," and sought enabling legislation from the state. The menace mounted until, in June, 1878, Noyes fled to Canada, as, thirty years before, he had fled from Vermont to Oneida. From a new home in Niagara Falls, Ontario, he continued to advise and inspire his old companions until his death on April 13, 1886.

With the Father's departure the community system collapsed. In August, 1879, complex marriage was abandoned. Most of the Oneidans paired off and married, to legitimize their children. There were distressing cases of mothers whose mates were already taken, of the children of Noyes himself, left high and dry. In the reorganization into conventional families it was necessary to establish rights of private property. As Noyes had foreseen, the demons of greed, self-seeking, jealousy, anger, and uncharitableness invaded the serene halls of the Mansion House.

The Oneida industries were converted into a joint-stock company, the shares distributed to the members of the community. After a period of drifting and fumbling, the enterprises came under the inspired management of Pierrepont Noyes and became a model of welfare capitalism, or partnership of owners and workers. To the present day, high wages are paid, profits are shared, and schools, country clubs, aids for home-building, are provided. Oneida is the leading producer of stainless-steel flatware, the second largest producer of silver-plated ware in the United States. It has over three thousand employees in the Oneida plants, and many more in the factories in Canada, Mexico, and the United Kingdom. Its net sales in 1967 amounted to fifty-four million dollars, its net profits to two and a half million.

This outcome is not the least surprising feature of the Oneida story. Nearly all other communistic experiments in this country have long since disappeared, leaving nothing more than a tumble-down barracks or a roadside marker. Oneida found a transformation into the capitalist world. It did so at the cost of losing its religious and social doctrines; but it has never lost the idealism, the humanitarianism, and the communitarian love of John Humphrey Noyes.

Mrs. Amelia J. Bloomer in bloomers

18 Mrs. Bloomer's Pantaloons à la Turk

arly in April, 1851, word from upstate reached New York City that Mrs. Amelia J. Bloomer of Seneca Falls had brazenly shown herself in a short dress and "trousers." Mrs. Bloomer was editress of *The Lily*, a monthly journal for women, which advocated temperance, women's rights, and general reform, combined with purity. The *New York Tribune* quoted the Syracuse *Standard:* "Several ladies appeared in the streets with dresses of a very *laconic* pattern, and pantaloons à la Turk. The new style looks decidedly tidy and neat, and imparts to the wearer quite a sprightly and youthful appearance." In the first days of May, great excitement was produced at Oswego Landing by two ladies in short Turkish dresses. Horace Greeley, the *Tribune*'s forward-looking editor, judged that a revolution in female costume was undoubtedly in preparation. On May 6, a wearer of the new dress was reported by the Auburn *Advertiser:* "She presented a fine appearance. . . . Her dress was decidedly rich, and made her appear more like a celestial being than one confined to earth. . . . We say, hurrah for the short dress and trowsers." And during the month of May, the reformed costume was noted by observers all the way from Lawrence,

Massachusetts, to Milwaukee.

The advocates of Turkish styles attacked New York City cautiously, creeping up on the metropolis through its outskirts. A pantalooned scout was glimpsed on the streets of Stamford, Connecticut, and another in Newark. The Brooklyn *Eagle* of May 29 told of a threat from the southeast: "Yesterday evening the idlers about the City Hall were agreeably surprised to observe a young lady, apparently in the bloom of her teens, and as beautiful as a boquet of roses, walk along Court Street; her limbs, which appeared symmetrical as the chiseled pedestals of a sculptured Venus, encased in a pair of yellow pantaloons, which displayed, peeping out from underneath, an ankle on which the closest scrutiny could discover no defect. She had on a short frock coat with rounded skirts and a neat little straw hat, sitting gracefully over a deluge of wavy curls. The young lawyers about these parts looked on approvingly, declaring such a dress well calculated to preserve the *constitution*."

The invasion of Manhattan began on June 5, when a young lady appeared on Broadway in the new dress, arousing more curiosity than hostility. The editor of the *Tribune* saw the costume with his own eyes. He described it as a short skirt, reaching a little below the knee, and wide Turkish trousers of plaid silk. The wearer attracted so much attention that she was forced to take refuge in a store until the crowd dwindled. "As we were going up Broadway at dusk," the editor continued, "we passed another specimen—a young lady, in a light dress of grayish color, made in the new style, walking with a gentleman. She appeared quite unembarrassed, and to our eyes her dress was picturesque and graceful."

Soon, however, the conservative spirit of the populace rallied against innovation. On June 26 it was reported that a pantalooned lady, walking up the Bowery with a gentleman, was followed by such a jeering crowd that, near Houston

Street, the pair took sanctuary in a milliner's shop, which was barred against the mob, while the police arrested two of the more violent critics. The lady and gentleman had clearly erred in venturing into the territory of those traditionalists, the "Bowery bhoys," who could brook no extravagance in dress. They themselves wore high beaver hats with the nap divided and brushed in opposite directions, gaudy silk neckcloths, black frock coats, and full pantaloons turned up at the bottom. They were not idlers and gangsters but apprentices who had a reputation for being formidable fighters and mockers and improvisers of insulting doggerels.

In the churches the clergy fought the innovators in their own manner, belaboring the reformers with texts. They made great play with Deut. XXII, 5: "The women shall not wear that which pertaineth unto a man, neither shall a man put on a woman's garment: for all that do so are abomination unto the Lord thy God." They recalled that the Lord himself had designed the first fashions: "Unto Adam also and to his wife did the Lord God make coats of skins, and clothed them." (Gen. III, 21). Mrs. Bloomer pertly answered that the text does not exclude the possibility of the Deity's designing bloomers.

Even the stage joined hands with the church to sustain the old against the new, and a farce entitled "The Bloomers, or Pets in Pants" was promptly produced. It was followed by a Bloomer Troupe of Minstrels, who performed at White's Melodeon, featuring groups of living model statuary. There was a Bloomer Parade at Barnum's Museum, and humorous playlets at other theatres.

Within two years the foes of the female trouser won the cause. The initiators of fashion turned to newer styles, while those who wore pantaloons as a matter of principle concluded that their costume was a hindrance to the more important reform of women's rights.

The historian of the bloomer might justifiably begin his

study of origins in the Garden of Eden, with the aprons, sometimes translated "breeches" ("*chagorah*" in the Hebrew), which Eve sewed of fig leaves. It would seem, however, that the reformers of 1851 were not inspired by our first parents. Perhaps some of these reformers had been stirred to dangerous dreams by the engravings of indolent trousered odalisques in Byron's voluptuous works. The horrid name of George Sand, shouted from pulpits as an example of French religious infidelity and moral looseness, evoked the picture of the authoress in turban, Turkish trousers, and *babouches*, smoking her narghile with Chopin. In France there was also the precedent of Hélène Marie Weber, a determined feminist and a writer of powerful essays demanding the emancipation of her sex. She was a practical farmer and went to market in man's attire with her produce. It was her contention that woman's physical development was impossible in the conventional dress; she wore, therefore, a dress coat and pantaloons of black cloth, and on full-dress occasions a dark blue dress coat, with plain flat gilt buttons, a waistcoat of buff cassimere, and drab pantaloons. She told her American sisters with complacency that her clothes were made by the best Paris tailors.

Nevertheless, it is most likely that the inspiration for the American reform came less from foreign sources than from the simple pantalet, commonly worn by small American girls during the forties and fifties. Sensible women looked on the free and modest dress of their daughters, and envied and wondered at what they saw.

They had good reason for envy. Fashion decreed the tiny waist, intolerable to busy and fecund women. Medical men spoke many a warning of the physical evils produced by tight lacing. From padded hips were hung layer after layer of petticoat and a silk skirt, lapped, pleated, and folded, of appalling weight. The female form, from the waist down, resembled an inverted artichoke.

About 1850 fashion invented a new cruelty, the trailing skirt. "Street-sweeper," it was nicknamed; the director of the London Crystal Palace affirmed that he employed his lady visitors to clean his floors. The style might pass in London and Paris, but in slovenly New York and the American village it was a comical calamity. Fine ladies on their way to church caught papers, refuse, and cigar butts in their wake, kept them in play for a few yards, and discharged them inopportunely. Elegant callers, in wet weather, entered with dripping trains and petticoats and apologetically shook burrs and straws from their stained ruffles. Most women, poor creatures, complained and submitted. There were many, however, who were in no mood for submission.

The question of women's wrongs and rights was then a subject of hot debate. Their wrongs, legal, economic, and social, were very real. Married women were wards in law and could not own property separately nor claim guardianship of their own children. They could not make contracts, sue or be sued, claim wages earned, or collect for damages done their persons or characters. Such distressing cases were cited as that of the Massachusetts gentleman who married an heiress with fifty thousand dollars. He died within a year and left his widow, by will, her own fifty thousand dollars on condition that she should not marry again. No professions were open to women except elementary teaching, and no trades except sewing and household work. No medical or professional schools admitted females, and no colleges except Oberlin, which, high-mindedly, accepted women and Negroes. Gentlemen boasted of American chivalry, but their chivalry was mingled with a scornful superiority which sometimes used a horsewhip as a corrective. The ladies asked for less chivalry and more justice.

As might have been expected, reform began in that curious strip of country across northern New York State where the spirit burned with a brighter flame than elsewhere. This was the holy land of abolition, prohibition, socialistic and communistic experiment, spiritualism, and a dozen novel religions, of which Mormonism is the greatest example. The fiery tempest of revivalism here scorched so many souls that the region was called "the burned-over district." Curiously enough, the limits of this ardent land coincide roughly with the Goitre Belt. Iodine has brought it health and has, perhaps, put an end to visions. The burned-over district now votes the straight Republican ticket.

In the hyperthyroid village of Seneca Falls lived a group of remarkable women, of whom Elizabeth Cady Stanton was the most remarkable. A sympathetic conversation between Mrs. Stanton and Lucretia Mott of Philadelphia, who was visiting in nearby Waterloo, resulted in the first Woman's Rights Convention, held in Seneca Falls, on July 19, 1848. Susan B. Anthony of Rochester was soon a convert, and other apostles of the movement also received their consecration.

Among them was Mrs. Amelia J. Bloomer, deputy postmistress of Seneca Falls and editress of *The Lily*, which she had begun as a woman's temperance magazine and had converted into the leading journal of feminism in America. Mrs. Bloomer was not the discoverer of the bloomer. She gave the dress its notoriety, and the world gave it her name, but the glory of first wearing the American trouser belongs to Mrs. Elizabeth Smith Miller.

Mrs. Miller was a cousin of Elizabeth Cady Stanton and the daughter of Gerrit Smith, eminent abolitionist and miscellaneous reformer of Peterboro, New York. It was apparently in the late autumn of 1850 that this memorable woman first sheared her flowing train and bifurcated the petticoat. Mrs. Stanton recorded her cousin's visit to Seneca Falls and wrote that Mrs. Miller was "dressed somewhat in the Turkish style— short skirt, full trousers of black broadcloth, a Spanish cloak, of the same material, reaching to the knee; beaver hat and feathers and dark furs; altogether a most becoming costume and exceedingly convenient for walking in all kinds of weather. To see my cousin, with a lamp in one hand and a baby in the other, walk upstairs with ease and grace, while, with flowing robes, I pulled myself up with difficulty, lamp and baby out of the question, readily convinced me that there was sore need of reform in woman's dress, and I promptly donned a similar attire. What incredible freedom I enjoyed for two years!"

Was the inspiration for the new costume Mrs. Miller's own? I suspect that the idea, if not the design, was that of her father, Gerrit Smith, that steady geyser of reform. At any rate, Mrs. Miller was the first and most constant of the trousered ladies. She wore the costume for seven years, during which her father served a term in Congress. She attended the most fashionable Washington dinners and receptions in her reformed dress, but she seems to have abandoned it when she settled with her husband in Geneva, New York, where the memory of her brilliant mind and warm heart is still cherished. She did not tell her Geneva friends of her bloomered days, or if she did, her friends have forgotten.

The example of Mrs. Miller and Mrs. Stanton was soon followed by Mrs. Bloomer. In March, 1851, she appeared in the new costume on the streets of Seneca Falls, a village blasé toward marvels. The reform was announced in the April number of *The Lily*.

Daring, discontented, uncomfortable women welcomed the bloomer with joy. The circulation of *The Lily* boomed; its editorial office bulged with requests for patterns. Corset-sore subscribers heeded gladly Mrs. Stanton's command: "We propose no particular costume; we say to you, at your firesides, ladies, unhook your dresses, and let everything hang loosely about you; now take a long breath, swell out as far as you can, and at that point fasten your clothes. Now please cut off those flowing skirts to your knees, and put on a pair of loose trousers buttoned about your ankle. Let us razee and correct our garments, until they assume their proper place; all standing out of the way of the full and perfect development of the woman."

Country women were particularly grateful. My own grandmother, a girl on a farm near Penn Yan, secretly made herself a bloomer dress and flaunted it before her shouting menfolk. It was wonderful for milking.

The costume at its worst was lacking in chic. Mrs. Stanton confesses that the reformers might better have taken as a model the flying folds of Diana the Huntress. Nevertheless the ensemble at its best could be rich and elegant. When Mrs. Bloomer addressed a meeting in New York in 1853, the *Tribune* described her wearing a dark-brown changeable tunic and a kilt descending just below the knees, the skirt of which was trimmed with black velvet. Her pantaloons were of the same texture and trimmed in the same style. She wore gaiters. Her headdress was cherry and black. Her dress had a large open corsage, with bands of velvet over the white chemisette, in which was a diamond stud pin. She wore flowing sleeves, tight undersleeves, and black lace mitts.

The only serious criticism which the reformers made of their own reform was that the light skirt, or kilt, was insufficiently ballasted. Mrs. Bloomer herself admitted: "The high winds played sad work with short skirts when I went out, and I was greatly annoyed and mortified by having my skirts turned over my head and shoulders on the streets."

The bloomer, launched by the women's righters as a symbol of women's right to reasonable comfort, gained at first because it connoted reform. The emancipated adopted the emancipated dress as a matter of course. They fancied that they were cutting off all ancient prejudice with their flounced trains. On the other hand, many tender females were repelled by the popular identification of bloomerism with radicalism. The extremists among the women's righters lent themselves, indeed, to ridicule. Such was Elizabeth Denton of Boston, the leader of the Female Seers, who taught that woman is of the nature of the cherub and the seraph while man's nature is that of the stallion and the dog. Such was Eliza Farnham of Staten Island, the female warden of Sing Sing, who in a curious volume proved by physiology the superiority of woman to man. "Woman's bust has a nobler contour, her bosom a finer swell." She also rebutted Darwin's statement that male rudimentary mammae are vestigial remnants; rather, she contended, the mammae are young buds of the future, promising that man shall flower, ages hence, in feminine perfection.

The soberer members of the women's party found such enthusiasts compromising to their cause. They were embarrassed also by the fact that male sympathizers with the movement wore, as a badge and banner, the shawl. They found that their bloomer dress, sensible though it was, distracted the attention of audiences from the serious business at issue. To the most weighty of arguments, the opposition replied only: "Men, women, and Bloomers! Faugh! Bah!"

The reformers persisted, nonetheless. They were heartened by the news that their fashion had caught on in England. The London *Guardian* reported, on August 13, 1851: "Two ladies were to be seen promenading Oxford Street on Saturday afternoon, attired in the Bloomer costume, and escorted by a crowd of ragged urchins and a number of the curious of both sexes. They were said to be mother and daughter, of the name of Jeffers, recently arrived in the metropolis to attend the vegetarian soirée. The ladies were attired in black satin *visites* and an inner tunic reaching a little below the waist; the inner garment being loose pink-striped pantaloons, fastened round the leg a little above the ankle; the headdress was of the usual kind. ... The mob at last got troublesome, and the ladies entered a cab, and were driven off, amidst shouts of laughter."

A Mrs. Dexter adopted the reform in England—an unfortunate sponsor, for, said the *Guardian*, "she is connected with the Socialists, and is well known to such reporters as have occasion to enter the vile dens of infidelity in the metropolis." She announced a lecture in costume but took fright at the disorderly audience and disappeared, together with the ticket seller and the gate money. A Bloomer Ball was held in Hanover Square; some six or seven hundred men and twenty-five women attended. "The ladies did not compose the élite of the casinos," said the ungallant *Guardian*. "The less that is said either of themselves or their dresses the better. . . . The whole tone and style of the thing smacked unmistakably of Vauxhall on a cheap night. . . . A battle royal raged in the supper room with pieces of bread and orange and jelly."

Punch fell upon the new style with gouty rage. At least two farces on the theme were produced. They are chiefly amusing today for their comical avoidance of the wicked word "trouser." "Would you believe it, ma'am, she actually wears the [pointing to her legs] the—the—thingummys, ma'am; and though her name's Porter, her dress is half-and-half." "No, ma'am, I'll stick to my native petticoats, and never wear the tr——, I mean, the mustn't-mention-'ems." The word "trouser" was more freely uttered in America than in England, as an observant Englishman noted in 1858. He recorded, on the other hand, that no genteel American lady would ask for the "breast" or the "leg" of a chicken. She was trained to the strange circumlocutions of "white meat" and "dark meat." (Indeed, only recently have "second joints" been publicly denominated "thighs" in the supermarkets.)

In the two hemispheres the bloomer began to drown in ridicule. The comics made their inevitable jokes. The churches uttered their anathemas. Hardest to bear, perhaps, was the journalists' air of humorous, fatherly superiority. Thus spoke a writer in the *Knickerbocker Magazine*: "Had this sacred veil, so long the chosen tabernacle of the well-turned ankle and the lithe and graceful limb, gone up by degrees and modestly slow;

nay, had the outer veil alone of the *santum sanctorum* been seized with an upward tendency, thereby displaying to public view only those elaborate and nameless embroideries which have been like desert-roses unseen by the eye of man, save when they tripped daintily across a stream, or were dexterously fillipped over a puddle, we might restrain our indignation and repress our frowns: but alas! the outer veil and the 'eleven inner veils' are all aspiring! all ascending! Now we await, with fear and trembling, the 'Excelsior!' the yet higher in ascent and the shorter in skirt, till at last woman, lovely woman, shorn of her glorious plumage, the silk, the satin, and the challé, fobbed of frill, furbelow, and flounce, shall stand confessed! perfection pantalooned! stiff as a lightning-rod, and awkward as little Johnny Sprouts in his first go-to-meeting swallow-tail!''

Under such onslaughts the bloomer fled. It took refuge, naturally enough, in the communities and conventicles of reform. It was commonly worn in Modern Times, Long Island. In the North American Phalanx near Red Bank, New Jersey, the prettiest girls were chosen for waitresses and wore knee-length kilts and trousers, and, about their heads, wreaths of leaves. According to visitors, they looked very elegant. At Father Noyes's Oneida Community a similar uniform was prescribed. The strong-minded ladies of Berlin Heights, a free-love colony near Cleveland, indicated their freedom by their dress. Artemus Ward, who amused our forefathers, thus described his visit to the colony: "The wimin was wuss than the men. They wore trowsis, short gownds, straw hats with green ribbins, and all carried bloo cotton umbrellers. Presently a perfeckly orful lookin female presented herself at the door. Her gownd was skanderlusly short, and her trowsis was shameful to behold."

One bold woman continued to flaunt her pantaloons before the great world. Dr. Mary Walker of Oswego and Washington, first lieutenant in the Medical Corps of the Union Army, wore them by the authority of a special Act of Congress. Her misadventures, her frequent arrests as she entered ladies' retiring rooms, would have disheartened a less courageous woman.

The bloomer, in fact, never entirely died. It led a furtive existence in sanitariums and the gymnasiums of girls' schools. When, in the late eighties, the safety bicycle came wavering down our streets, the bloomer reappeared in glory, a symbol of woman set free, bestriding the machine of the new age.

And today the humorous, fantastic fears of 1850 are realized. Mrs. Bloomer's name is immortalized in English speech. The thingummies, the mustn't-mention-'ems, have become commonplaces and in their turn have aspired and ascended. Woman, lovely woman, stands confessed.

Josiah Warren

19 Josiah Warren
and Modern Times, L. I.

Passengers on the Greenport line of the Long Island Railroad in the 1850's dozed their way through Hicksville, Farmingdale, and Deer Park. They were then likely to rouse a little as the conductor announced, with a politely sarcastic inflexion, the station of Modern Times. Ill-bred travelers were known to add, aloud, "Where no child knows his own father."

The passengers stared through grimy windows at the bleak station, set in the midst of scrub oak (or shrub oak, as they said in the fifties), and the dreary waste levels of Long Island sumac and barberry stretching afar. Peering abroad, they were rewarded by a glimpse of the notorious philosophers, lean men, with the long hair that was then the badge of progress, the pride of the intellectual Samson. Or, lucky enough to espy the philosophers' ladies, they nudged and clucked at the lascivious bloomer, at skirts which flaunted the ankle's shame. There was one May Day when the children of Modern Times greeted the train by forming a tableau on the station platform beneath a defiant banner which read, "We are Individuals."

Some of the passengers were aware that Modern Times was a community of idealists, who pretended to nothing less than a regeneration of the human spirit in a better world. Their one essential doctrine was that of Individual Sovereignty, or philosophical anarchy; their common enemy, the moral and social restrictions of organized society. Having abolished tradition, they were able to reorganize human life on a basis of pure reason. Money was discarded, and with it the woes that money makes. Their economics was founded on labor; their currency represented labor hours. Every man sought his own salvation, and the world's, in his own way. Some found it in religion, in Swedenborgianism, Comtism, spiritualism, mesmerism; some in women's rights, coeducation, equality for women in political suffrage and in costume; some in pacifism; some in the Water Cure, or drenching of the body, externally and internally, with healing floods; some in abstinence from alcohol and tobacco; some in vegetarianism and the bread and crackers of Dr. Sylvester Graham. One woman was so constant in her dietary faith as to die after a year's exclusive regime of beans without salt. One colonist advocated the plurality of wives; one, nudity; many, freedom of the affections and the abolition of marriage. And, such is the quality of the human mind, the doctrine of Free Love (or Free Lust, as snorting editors rephrased it) captured the imagination of the outside world to the exclusion of the doctrines in politics, economics, and religion. Even today the mention of Modern Times arouses only the connotation of Free Love among those who dwell upon its ruins, in the smiling village of Brentwood, L. I.

The village of Modern Times was the creation of Josiah Warren, one of those early-nineteenth-century Yankees who united idealism, versatility, and more than a touch of genius. Born in Boston in 1798, he removed to Cincinnati about 1818, and gained local fame as an orchestra leader. He invented and manufactured with much success a lamp which burned lard instead of tallow. In 1824 he met the social reformer Robert Owen. A ready convert to Owen's Communism, he sold his lamp factory and joined his mentor's community at New Harmony, Indiana. Communism he soon found uncongenial, because of its suppression of individuality, initiative, and personal responsibility. He concluded that all future reform must be based on individual liberty.

Warren returned to Cincinnati, where he established a Time Store, the model for the Time Store we shall find in operation in Modern Times. He was busy also with inventions in the field of stereotyping and printing. He built the first cylinder press, antedating the Hoe press by five years. His machine used a continuous roll of paper, a device commonly credited to Bullock in 1865. Warren's press was used to print the Evansville, Indiana, *South-Western Sentinel* in 1840, but the printers, recognizing its menace to their employment, repeatedly damaged it, until Warren, in a fury, destroyed it without having obtained a patent. The stone press bed was in 1906 the doorstep of a house in New Harmony.

Warren established the villages of Equity and Utopia in Ohio, and developed in practice his theories of the Equity Movement. He came to New York in 1850, and soon gained support among the city's advanced thinkers for his project of an ideal community. He was described at this period as a short, thick-set man, with a bright, restless blue eye and nervous gestures. He was fluent and eager in conversation, and entirely absorbed in his social ideas. But one of the Modern Times colonists admitted that Warren was a poor speaker, and so sensitive that after a public wrangle he would retire to his house for as much as six weeks.

His doctrines were social and economic. He held that all government is evil, as it suppresses the individual, and the individual must be sovereign. He wanted no laws and no police. Men might unite for defense or common enterprises, but such combinations must be voluntary. The law of supply and demand would impel individuals to organize water and gas systems, asylums, and all the services of civilization. Religion and morals are the individual's affair. But no free man has the right to interfere with another's freedom, and all his actions are performed at his own cost. He cannot lay any of his own responsibility on society. And no one has the right to determine another's conduct unless he must bear the cost of the other's conduct.

Warren's economic theories begin with a thorough condemnation of the money system. Profit is taking something without giving an equivalent, interest is only plunder, and wealth an organized system of robbery. Money is a convention, a mere document. We are accustomed to setting a price on a commodity by calculating its value to the purchaser. But this is the transfer of the principle of war and conquest to the commercial world. By making value the governor of price, we make falsehood and hypocrisy the basis of trade, we make the rich richer and the poor poorer, we create trade for trade's sake and augment the number of non-producers, whose support is chargeable to labor; we degrade the dignity of labor, we prevent the scientific adjustment of supply to demand, we render competition destructive and desperate, and make the introduction of new machinery a calamity instead of a blessing.

"Cost the limit of price" was the slogan of Modern Times. Warren defined "cost" as all the sacrifices entailed in the production of a commodity, measured by the time and the repugnance of the labor involved. He would prove by experience that the substitution of cost price for value price would cure all the economic ills and injustices of the world.

Clearly, the new world would require a method of measuring labor and a circulating medium. Warren chose for Modern Times the production of corn as a standard, reckoning sixteen pounds of corn the normal equivalent of an hour's labor. On this basis he issued labor notes, promises to pay in personal service. These notes became the money, or circulating medium, of the village. Some of them are preserved, with other interesting memorials of Modern Times, in the Suffolk County Historical Society.

The financial and commercial center of Modern Times was the Time Store. The goods were marked at the cost price in American money, plus 4 per cent for overhead. The wholesalers' bills were publicly displayed to confound the suspicious. Conspicuous on the wall hung a large clock, and beneath the clock a dial, lettered with the day's hours and minutes. A customer entered and fingered, perhaps, the pile of Kentucky blue jean. The storekeeper, on addressing the customer, set the dial according to the clock. He showed the goods, displayed their virtues, and provided sales talk and local news as required. The sale completed, he consulted clock and dial, and found that the customer had consumed, perhaps, fifteen minutes of his time. He charged the customer the cost of the goods in money, plus 4 per cent for overhead, plus fifteen minutes in labor notes. He was ready to make change in his own promises to pay with his own labor or in the promises of others, which had accumulated in his till. These labor notes did not all have the same value in corn. The blacksmith's notes, for instance, had a higher purchasing value than the doctor's, for the blacksmith plied the more arduous and less interesting trade. The accumulation of negotiable labor notes made the Time Store a labor market. The notes of some, notoriously laggard and shiftless, depreciated in value and were finally refused, while others commanded a premium.

Clustering about the Time Store stood the village of Modern Times. Visitors described it as a pleasing settlement of a hundred modest cottages, painted a cheerful green and white, and surrounded by thriving vegetable gardens and abundant flowers. The sandy soil had responded well to cultivation and care. A certain bleakness of aspect was due to the absence of trees. But today the saplings planted in Modern Times opulently shade the homes of Brentwood.

No church spire rose above the village. Churches can hardly thrive where every man is a preacher and few will be the congregation. There was, for instance, Henry Edger, a composer, director of the glee club, and leader of the orchestra. He preached Positivism, or Comtism, or the Religion of Humanity of Auguste Comte, and celebrated Positive Festivals in a lecture room adjoining his log cabin. One of his printed sermons is dated the 24th Gutemberg, 75; the Comtists reformed the calendar with the faith. He seems to have made only two converts in the course of his ministry. Josiah Warren harbored the darkest of suspicions against him, believing him to be a Jesuit detailed to work against his Equity movement.

Sunday assemblies of a dimly religious character were held in the meetinghouse. Such a service began with the singing of "There's a Good Time Coming" and was followed by readings from the Bible and from Emerson's essays, a prayer to the Great Spirit, a hymn ("When the Might with the Right / And the Truth shall be"), and a sermon on the eventual enthronement of science.

Plays were presented fortnightly in this meetinghouse, and concerts frequently. The hall served also for dancing, to which the colonists were much given, and for gymnastics. The more beautiful and graceful sports were in vogue; a football game was once essayed, but it was abandoned as being too violent for philosophers.

Education was, as always, the concern of radical thinkers. It was proposed to educate children according to their special aptitudes, to train the emotions and passions for good, to establish coeducation of the sexes. An imposing Educational Institute was planned, and a roofless and windowless building christened "The College." The vaulting dreams took concrete form only in an elementary school and in a Mechanical College, in which Mr. Warren, the faculty, taught printing, stereotyping, brickmaking, bricklaying, carpentry, and music.

The principle of individual sovereignty found its richest application in the women's costumes. Some wore bloomers, some the outright pantaloon. More chose the dress of operatic peasants—the bouffant skirt to the knee and white stockings. The men showed less originality. One, indeed, advocated the total abolition of clothing and, under the rules of individual freedom, publicly practiced his faith. But he was looked at, it seems, askance. There was none who, like a member of the North American Phalanx at Red Bank, New Jersey, emerged from his earth bath to don a squeaky suit of tin.

Where thought and action are free, it is natural that the marriage bond should be subject to severe strains and torques. Some of the colonists had found refuge from unhappy unions in the tolerance of Modern Times. Others were led to a scorn of marriage by purely rational processes. While the majority lived according to a respectable domestic routine, all were trained to a large benevolence. "Folks ask no questions," said a villager. "We do not believe in life partnerships when the partners live unhappily. Everyone knows his own interest best. We don't interfere. The individual is sovereign and independent." A visitor reported that it was not thought polite to inquire about the parentage of newly born children, or to ask about the husband or wife of an individual. Temporarily married couples wore a red string around the finger in place of a ring. The disappearance of the string served as the ceremony and publication of divorce.

It is not, perhaps, commonly remembered today that in the Puritan mid-century the doctrine and practice of Free Love had many devotees. The movement had its colonies, its public advocates, its philosophers, and its martyrs. I find significant a convert's memory of his vows, shouted above the amorous thunders of Niagara Falls: "At the foot of Niagara's reef of rainbows, baptized by the mists of heaven, we pledged ourselves to unite our destinies, and work together for human welfare, so long as it was mutually agreeable." A disgruntled colonist of Modern Times, who had lost his money and his wife to his fellow-philosophers, warned the *New York Tribune* that a large circle of Free Lovers in New York City were covertly proselytizing, and preparing to throw off the mask of secrecy and defy public opinion.

Though Warren himself disapproved of mingling sex with economics, two of his lieutenants advocated the freedom of the affections. Dr. Thomas Low Nichols, proprietor of a water cure in Port Chester and an author of much merit, printed in his *Esoteric Anthropology* (1853) a catalogue of names for the reciprocal use of affinity-hunters all over the country. His removal from Port Chester to Modern Times was hastened by the accusation that he was putting esoteric anthropology in practice in his American Hydropathic Institute. "This is the philosophy of the brothel!" wrote an angry Port Chesterian to the *New York Tribune*.

More moderate in his views was Josiah Warren's principal backer, Stephen Pearl Andrews. This remarkable man had led a remarkable career, fighting slavery in Louisiana and Texas at the risk of his life, intriguing to involve Great Britain in slavery abolition in Texas, introducing Pitman's shorthand to America, writing books on the Chinese language, devising a universal language, Alwato, and erecting an inexplicable explanation of everything, which he named "Universology." His Order of Recreation held its meetings in a loft at 555 Broadway in New York until outraged public opinion forced the police to a spectacular raid. But visitors to this primitive love nest testify that the proceedings were entirely respectable. An inquisitive Frenchman noted that the women wore trousers, short skirts, tippets, and round hats. "All the women I met there were thin, ugly, old, and endowed with detestably shrill voices. They love to expatiate, and enjoy disparaging married men and marriage. But, in the matter of marriage, one must always be cautious of the opinions of thin, ugly, shrill old maids."

Andrews later rented four brownstone fronts on East Fourteenth Street and established a Unitary Home, or Pantarchy, of which he was the Great Pantarch. Warren's economic principles were there put into practice, with such success that the current costs of board and room were cut in half. Edmund Clarence Stedman, famous, not long ago, as a poet, lived in the Pantarchy, and in old age remembered with affection his bizarre fellow-boarders and the two-cent soups, the five-cent roasts, the three-cent desserts.

One of the Modern Times settlers, Dr. Edward Newberry, the colony's dentist, homeopathic physician, and phrenologist, held views at the opposite extreme from Free Love. These opinions he inherited from his father, who must have been one of the first of eugenists. The father, an Englishman, developed his theories of eugenics, then found a mate to fit his principles of breeding. By her he sired eighteen children. When she died, wrote a member of Modern Times in his unpublished memorials, "he sought just such another, who continued the good work so well begun." She gave her husband nineteen more children and, having exceeded the record of her predecessor, died content. Edward was the first of the second series of children. At the age of five he had a vision, revealing his motto throughout life: "Be ye perfect." Docile to revelation, he pursued perfection for himself and for the human race. He believed in the improvement of humanity by scientific cross-fertilization. Scorning the blind impulse called "falling in love," he proposed the union of the sexes by temperamental opposites, by an authoritative matching of the blond with the brunette, the muscular temperament with the nervous, the bilious with the locomotive. It would seem that he gained few adherents.

With such representatives of varied convictions, the chief product of Modern Times was evidently conversation. The accounts of intelligent visitors make clear that a lush crop of ideas flourished on the Long Island sands. Many of the ideas are exactly those which we complacently regard as modern. The proud name of the village was not ill chosen, after all.

Modern Times failed, like most experimental machines in a world lubricated by habit. It failed economically because the village had no industry but agriculture, and it needed more imports than it could pay for with exports. (A converted cigarmaker was forbidden to ply his noxious trade.) Modern Times failed socially because humanity has not virtue to meet the high demands of anarchy. One of the philosophers, a foe to all regulation, abandoned his faith when he was appointed to the New York police force. Others were tempted away by opportunities for profit in the contemptible currency of the United States. Dr. Nichols confessed sadly, "It was very well to teach that profit was plunder, and that to be rich only gave the power to rob others with impunity, that marriage was legalized adultery, and families petty despotisms. There were few who could resist the temptations to live upon the labor of others, and to preside over a despotism that society has stamped with respectability and power."

The anti-Free Love agitation, the panic of 1857, and the outbreak of the Civil War dealt successive blows to the community's health. Most of the founders departed to seek their salvations elsewhere. By 1862 the bloomers of Modern Times were shrouded in the petticoats of Brentwood.

Today, in the green avenues of Brentwood, the mention of Modern Times evokes the dimpled smile or the knowing leer. "Sure! It was a free-love colony!" is the villagers' response. Forgotten is all the idealism, the purpose of economic and social deliverance; remembered is the old bucolic envy which made of Modern Times the dreamland of its own wantonness. "I used to sneak downstairs and listen to my father and the section foreman," said a venerable resident of Brentwood. "And the section foreman, he told my father that when those Modern Timesers was going out a-huckleberrying, one of them would say to the other, 'You take my wife and I'll take yours!' Hih, hih, hih! 'You take my wife and I'll take yours!' That's what he says! 'You take my wife and I'll take yours!' " He gobbled with ancient glee.

Fitz Hugh Ludlow

20 Fitz Hugh Ludlow, the Hasheesh Eater

The name of Fitz Hugh Ludlow is cherished at Union College as the author of its sweet alma mater and of the popular "Terrace Song." In the literary history of the United States he has secured a brief footnote as a writer of fiction and miscellanies. Of these, the most celebrated and most interesting are his confessions of his lifelong addiction to hashish. Today no one needs to be told that hashish, *cannabis indica*, is a close relative of marijuana, pot, or grass.

Fitz Hugh Ludlow was born in New York on September 11, 1836. His father, the Reverend Henry Ludlow, became a Presbyterian pastor in Poughkeepsie. Fitz Hugh entered Princeton as a junior in 1854. When Nassau Hall burned in 1855, scattering the Princetonians, he transferred to Union as a junior. At Union he was respected for his facility in verse writing, and was apparently popular, though with reservations. He seemed often strange, exalted.

He had begun taking hashish even as a youth in Poughkeepsie. By the time he reached Union, he was possessed by the angel of the drug. She had brought him, in the beginning, poetic ecstasy and blissful Oriental visions; she now revealed herself as a hideous afreet, who drowned him in nightly horrors.

He looked to a literary career, but dared not affront the un-
certainties and distresses of New York's Grub Street. On his
graduation in 1856 he became a teacher of the classics and of English literature at the Watertown Academy in New York State.
Before entering on his duties he happened on an article in *Putnam's Magazine* by another slave of hashish, who told how, by
a fierce effort of will, he had cast off the habit. Ludlow wrote to
him and received from him advice and comfort. He tells how,
in agony and desperation, he succeeded in releasing himself from
the toils of his drug. He had to devise his own therapeutic
methods; they included excessive smoking and a kind of self-
hypnosis induced by blowing soap bubbles.

He describes his year in Watertown as a hell of nervous
torture, dreadful nightmares, and the correction of student
themes. According to the old device of the literary man, he
exorcised the evil spirit by writing a book about it. An excerpt,
"The Apocalypse of Hasheesh," appeared in *Putnam's Magazine* in December, 1856. In the same year he called on George
William Curtis, occupant of the Editor's Easy Chair of *Harper's
Magazine*, to question him about a writer's career. Curtis was
attracted to the "slight, bright-eyed, alert" young man; he de-
picted all the miseries of the literary life, but Ludlow remained
incredulous.

His book, *The Hasheesh Eater*, a substantial volume of 371
pages, was published by *Harper's* in the latter part of 1857. It
gained a resounding success. "He held the town in his slender
right hand at one time," recalls a literary lady, Mrs. M. E. W.
Sherwood.

His ill health prevented him from enjoying his celebrity to
the full. In 1858 he took the water cure and was treated for
serious nervous troubles. In a letter of January, 1859, he insists
(was it then necessary to insist?) that he has conquered his
"habits of stimulus," even the habit of smoking.

In 1858 we find him in New York, studying law and writing for the newspapers and magazines. Though he was admitted to the bar, he did not practice, but devoted himself for the rest of his life to journalism and free-lance writing. Hugh Charles Sebastian, who has written a valuable study of Ludlow in the form of a master's thesis for the University of Chicago, has located about twenty of his short stories, mostly in *Harper's Magazine* and the *Atlantic Monthly*. There were also topical and travel articles; a novel, *The New Partner in Clingham & Co., Bankers*, serialized in *Harper's*; a humorous series in *Vanity Fair*; a dramatization of *Cinderella*. Some of the stories appeared in book form.

In 1862 or earlier Ludlow married Rosalie H. Osborne of Waterford, New York. We know nothing of her beyond the fact that Mrs. T. B. Aldrich found her winsome and beautiful. The couple were members of a literary circle of which Bayard Taylor was the center and E. C. Stedman, T. B. Aldrich, and Richard Henry Stoddard important points on the circumference. In the several volumes of reminiscence and recollection by frequenters of this happy salon, I find Ludlow mentioned as among those present, usually just before "etcetera." He is recalled invariably as "The Hasheesh Eater." He seems to have been always a background figure. He was of course young, and I suspect shy, insecure, and unhappy.

His marriage was brief and unsuccessful. The pair were divorced, apparently before the California journey of 1863. We can only guess at the reasons. Several testimonies allege that in moments of stress Ludlow returned to his hashish, perhaps to more powerful drugs.

In 1863 Ludlow set off for a year-long journey to the Pacific Coast. His companion was Albert Bierstadt, probably America's most successful painter of the day—financially successful, that is. He sold his *Lander's Peak* for $25,000. When state legislatures or financial barons ordered a picture, they were likely to specify that it had to be a Bierstadt. Robert Louis Stevenson, in *The Wrecker*, has his gross millionaire mention Bierstadt as the symbol of art. Naturally the critics have taken their revenge. But today there is an upsurge of critical interest in Bierstadt and his congeners, and a notable rise of prices of their work.

Albert Bierstadt married the divorced wife of Fitz Hugh Ludlow. One would be tempted to see some hidden drama in this tangle of marriage, divorce, and friendship were it not that the marriage of Bierstadt and Mrs. Ludlow did not take place until 1886, sixteen years after Ludlow's death.

Ludlow and Bierstadt made their western journey by rail to Atchison, Kansas, thence by stagecoach and on horseback. In San Francisco they met the remarkable band of young writers who gathered in the office of *The Golden Era*, among them Bret Harte, Joaquin Miller, and Mark Twain. Ludlow impressed them by his ebullient speech, by his learning in many fields, including science, and by his fervent advocacy of the new Darwinian theory of evolution. His friends subjected him to a mock trial for heresy. Ludlow, with the *Origin of Species* under his arm, "testified in polysyllables to an amazed court and obtained a verdict of acquittal." Mark Twain humbly submitted his literary efforts to Ludlow for advice and correction, though Twain was only a year younger than Ludlow. And Twain wrote in a private letter that Ludlow had encouraged him to do something better than ephemeral journalism. Ludlow made several contributions to *The Golden Era*. In his "Goodbye Article" (November 22, 1863), he praised a number of local writers, saying of Twain that "he is a school by himself."

From San Francisco Ludlow pushed north to the Columbia River. In his account of the journey he mentions suffering from "pulmonary spasms." His biographer, Sebastian, sees in the phrase, with good reason, an indication of the tuberculosis which was to cause his death.

Again in New York, Ludlow published a travel book on his visit to the West. He continued to write and publish, but he seems to have dropped out of the literary gossip of the later sixties. Perhaps his divorce was looked upon coldly by the high-minded intelligentsia. Or, more likely, his tuberculosis worsened and he was simply too ill to bear the strain of social life.

In December, 1867, he married Maria O. Milliken, widow of Judge Milliken of Augusta, Maine. I can find no facts about her, but I have the fancy that she was less wife than mother and ministering angel, and I am pretty sure that she had some money, for in June, 1870, Ludlow, his wife, his sister, and his stepson went to Switzerland to seek health in the high mountains. He got no farther than Geneva. There he died, on September 12, 1870. He was one day over thirty-four years of age. Later his body was brought back to Poughkeepsie for burial.

It was a short, unhappy, blundering life. The promise which his classmates and teachers at Union saw in him was hardly fulfilled. His youthful addiction to hashish certainly mined his health and prepared the way for the fatal tuberculosis. His early marriage and divorce must have worked havoc with his sensitive nature. His one real success was his first book. A youthful triumph, never repeated, is a literary man's incubus.

It would be pleasant to report that Ludlow was an extraordinary writer, a genius unsuspected. I fear I cannot do so. His stories seem to me terrible. They are echoes of all the other magazine stories of his time, originating in literature, not life, conducted with no regard for truth and with little for verisimilitude. His travel sketches are far better. He was an excellent observer and reporter. He sought out the novel and the quaint; he writes with pleasant gusto, though with much abuse of a ready-made poetic vocabulary, as self-consciously picturesque as Bierstadt's paintings.

The best of his works certainly is *The Hasheesh Eater.* Here is a sincerity and reality that he could not recapture when he tried to construct stories solely from his imagination. A considerable part of his book consists of descriptions of his drug-prompted hallucinations. These have both a clinical and a poetic quality. Ludlow renders well the remarkable sharpening of perception the drug confers, the tremendous enlargement of space and time. He finds lyric phrasing to convey the unearthly beauty of his visions and the unearthly horror of the evil fantasia which succeeded his bliss. He is a psychedelic Dante in reverse, descending from the Paradiso to the Inferno. His descriptions, drawing from his subconscious a strange mingling of the sublime and the grotesque, often suggest the work of Dali and other surrealists. The writer's passion gives his work an intensity which the reader recognizes and sympathetically feels. This is a very considerable literary achievement.

Fitz Hugh Ludlow will remain dear to Union men as long as they sing his alma mater, one of the few which express an elevated idea with poetic and rhythmical competence and one of the few which do not inspire a horrid vertigo in the sensitive reader. One may wonder why Ludlow, possessed in youth of so much of the imagination and technical skill of the poet, did not later distinguish himself in the field of verse. The reason, I suspect, is that he tried to live by literature, and that his pot-boiling stories and articles left him no time for the filing and chiseling of verse, which is so time destroying and so ill paid. He wrote only a few poems, and most of the surviving examples are not really very good. There is one, however, which renders, with a humorous air and with technical virtuosity, his grievance against life. He makes his confession with a smile, burlesquing himself, but at the same time revealing himself and his truth. Let his "Too Late" serve as his own epitaph on his pitiful, doomed life.

> There sat an old man on a rock
>   And unceasing bewailed him of Fate—
> That concern where we all must take stock,
>   Though our vote has no bearing or weight;

And the old man sang him an old, old song;
Never sang voice so clear and strong
That it could drown the old man's for long,
    For he sang the song "Too late! Too late!"

When we want, we have for our pains
    The promise that if we but wait
Till the want has burned out of our brains,
    Every means shall be present to state;
        While we send for the napkin the soup gets cold,
        While the bonnet is trimming the face grows old,
        When we've matched our buttons the pattern is sold,
            And everything comes too late—too late!

. . .

Ah! now, though I sit on a rock,
    I have shared one seat with the great;
I have sat—knowing naught of the clock—
    On love's high throne of state;
        But the lips that kissed, and the arms that caressed
        To a mouth grown stern with delay were pressed,
        And circled a breast that their clasp had blessed,
            Had they only not come too late—too late!

Dr. Holt, armed with two pistols, wounded J. P. Morgan (above) twice before the two-hundred-and-twenty-pound millionaire succeeded in bringing him down

21 Dr. Frank Holt,
the Scholarly Assassin

Erich Muenter, A.B. (University of Chicago, '99), alias Frank Holt, A.B. (Fort Worth Polytechnic College, '09), Ph.D. (Cornell, '14), was the only man I ever knew who had two university careers under two different names, who presumably poisoned his wife, and who beyond doubt dynamited a room in the Capitol Building at Washington and later shot J. P. Morgan in the hip and groin. The two of us, Muenter and I, were in a class in Old French together at Cornell in 1913, when he was preparing his doctor's thesis. He was a man in his thirties, tall, thin, and hawk-faced, given to staring out of the window. I remember especially his habit of sucking his teeth, in what I later recognized was a vampirish manner, whenever he had made a happy translation from Chrétien de Troyes. He had a faint lisp and a gangling walk. He jingled coins in his pocket a good deal. Indeed, he was very conscious of money, and, through the agency of a For Exchange column of ads in the Ithaca *Journal*, did an elaborate business in second-hand articles such as wastebaskets, office desks, student lamps, and typewriters. As far as I know, these deals were honest and were made profitable for Muenter only because of the keen trading sense he seemed to possess. He was not popular on the campus. People avoided walking home with him. He commonly wore a felt hat pulled down over his eyes. He was somber and aloof.

After he blew up the room in the Capitol and shot J. P. Morgan in the hip and groin, I took more interest in the past life of this colleague than I had in his existence when we sat side by side in the Old French class. I talked with people who had known him at Cornell and with people who had known him before that at Harvard, where he was believed to have poisoned his wife. Later on I wrote to people who were said to have known him in other years, and I received illuminating replies from some of them. I have decided to put all these things together as a moral tale for the instruction of a new generation of college students, the moral being: *Watch your classmates, fellows*.

Erich Muenter was born in Germany, apparently around 1880. He came to America in his teens, studied at the University of Chicago, and taught in the Chicago public schools and in the University of Kansas. He went to Harvard in 1904 as an instructor in German, taking with him his wife and small daughter. He was interested in occultism and was said to have formed a secret society for the study of medieval mysteries. He was supposed to have held that he could liberate his soul from his body and that after death the soul could be set free from its tenement by cremation.

The Muenter home seemed to be the abode of harmony and sentiment. Guests at the family's musical evenings were favorably impressed by the host's demonstrations of affection for his wife.

On April 10, 1906, she gave birth to a second child. In attendance were only one or two Christian Science practitioners and her husband. Two Cambridge physicians, Dr. McIntire and Dr. Taylor, had declined the case after differences with the Christian Science practitioners.

On April 16, Mrs. Muenter died. The husband alone was present at the time of her death. Muenter summoned Dr. Taylor. Supposedly as a matter of mere routine, Dr. Taylor did not sign a death certificate. An autopsy was performed by the medical examiner, Dr. Swan of Cambridge. Dr. Swan gave the cause of death as an aftereffect of childbirth, but, perhaps because of some faint suspicion, sent the contents of her stomach to the Harvard Medical College for examination.

Muenter afterward received his wife's body from the medical examiner and accompanied it to Chicago, taking with him his week-old baby and the older child. In Chicago, Mrs. Muenter's remains were cremated and the children were turned over to his brother-in-law. Erich Muenter then disappeared.

The Harvard Medical College was in no particular hurry about the examination of the stomach's contents. When the technicians got around to it, they were astonished to find that Mrs. Muenter's stomach was full of arsenic. The District Attorney was informed, and the press. A nationwide search for Muenter began. Harvard, which had not had a faculty murder since Professor Webster of the Chemistry Department killed Dr. George Parkman in 1849, was profoundly stirred.

Muenter's brothers-in-law talked freely. They suspected, and the reporters turned the suspicions into facts, that Muenter had another wife living in Germany. They told of several occasions when open gas jets flooded the Muenter home. They had no doubt that Muenter had murdered their sister. The obvious difficulty about this supposition was that there was no direct evidence.

Muenter, in some hiding place, read the newspapers and was filled with indignation. To the various accusations made against him, he made a remarkable rebuttal. He either had some amateur print or himself printed a pamphlet entitled *A Protest*. Copies were mailed from New Orleans, on June 2, to his old Harvard colleagues and to certain of his friends and enemies.

In *A Protest* he chose to confute the accusations against him by the method of burlesque. He began with extravagant humor a narrative of wife-poisoning and autopsy-performing at a hypothetical university. The pamphlet then launched into a fervent attack on the press for its publication of crime news. The printing of such news made the public callous and gave it a morbid taste for sensation, the author asserted. He appealed to citizens, civic federations, social workers, and labor leaders to raise the tone of the press. He then upbraided society for its mistreatment of the criminal and asked that our system of laws, a relic of the Roman system of revenge upon the ill-doer, give way to Christian teaching. The community was in fact the great criminal. It should overwhelm the wrongdoer with love; it should replace prisons with schools for the erring. "And if my fellow-men call this protest of mine insanity, then I will spend the rest of my life on my knees and beg the merciful Father in Heaven to take away all the rest, if need be, but to leave me my insanity."

Muenter then addressed his brothers-in-law directly, with a mingling of supplication and reproach. He insisted that they could not understand his relations with his dead wife, with whom he was still in spiritual communication. His married life, he said, was "complicated"; it contained "a sacred secret." He planned to write an account of it for specialists in psychological research. "The whole matter has merely scientific interest, and for scandal-mongers and sensation-hunters who have no scientific interests it will not be available."

As far as I can learn, the account for the psychologists was never written.

Erich Muenter continued to live his new life undetected. Under the name of Frank Holt, he went to Mexico and worked as a stenographer in a branch office of Krupp, the great German steel and armament firm, and for various mining companies. After a time he recrossed the border into Texas and laboriously made a new existence and a new personality. He entered the Fort Worth Polytechnic Institute as a freshman in February, 1908, and made such astounding progress that he was awarded an A.B. in June of the following year. While speeding through the curriculum, he found time to teach German in the college and to woo and marry a classmate, a minister's daughter. The union was blessed with two children. Confident of his destiny, he greatly increased the risk of exposure by resuming his old trade of college teacher of German. He dared even to come to Cornell, which enjoys some social contacts with Harvard. He attended the 1912 summer school, and was appointed instructor in German in 1913. He worked for his Ph.D. in his spare time. That was when I sat next to him in the Old French class. His acceptance of this risk apparently proved to him his superiority to common men and to fate.

In the end, he was actually recognized. A professor from the University of Chicago, doing some brief research in Cornell's famous Icelandic Collection, got the notion that he had seen Holt before. The visitor observed Holt's characteristic lisp, his loose-jointed way of walking. He then mentally superimposed handle-bar mustaches and an educator's Vandyke on Holt's clean-shaven face. "Your Holt," he said to a Cornell colleague, "is Erich Muenter!"

Though the Cornell colleague had once met Muenter, it had never occurred to him that the inoffensive Holt might be the Harvard fiend. A hard dilemma confronted the two teachers. To denounce or not to denounce? They discussed the ethical point involved. To be sure, they did not know all the facts of the Harvard *cause célèbre*. They were aware that Muenter had never been indicted or tried and that his legal and moral guilt was not established. They were moved by sympathy for Holt's new wife and his two children.

"I decided not to expose him," the Chicago professor wrote to the newspapers afterward, freely admitting, and defending, his action. "He seemed to be getting along nicely and to be a credit to the department. . . . The man had experienced a really tragic fate and was trying to do right."

Holt's manner toward the Chicago professor told that he knew he was recognized and that he appealed silently for silence. The visitor recalled, in a letter to me: "Holt's attitude, whenever I saw him, was one of the utmost self-assurance. The only time he seemed to quail and wish to avoid my glance was when I saw him across the street helping his wife and child into a streetcar. I imagine his nerve temporarily failed him. My nerve sometimes was a bit shaky late on winter nights when I was going from the library building home to my room, when the streets and bridges and canyon walls of the campus were covered with ice, and I reflected how easy it would be for a determined man with a guilty secret to knock the possessor of the secret down a declivity in such a manner that the latter would never tell the secret. I was always glad when I got out on level ground, if there is any in Ithaca. I was always glad of the company of the campus bulldog, Napoleon, when he happened to be going my way."

In the first year of World War I, Holt showed his pro-German sympathies in a letter to the Ithaca *Journal*, asking fair play for Germany and a ban on the shipment of munitions to the Allies. But he was counted a moderate in comparison with Professor Davidsen, who left Cornell to take an executive post with the German government, or Professor Flügel, formerly a German army officer. When Professor Flügel borrowed a good deal of money and left town, Professor Thilly of the Philosophy Department made a pun still cherished in faculty circles. "*Mein Geld hat Flügel genommen!*" said Professor Thilly.

Dr. Holt was, it seemed, secure. He got his Ph.D. and received an appointment as professor and head of the Department of Modern Languages in a Southern sectarian university. Early in June, 1915, he concluded his business for the scholastic year at

Cornell. In a farewell call on a professor of Romance languages, he said happily that he had been chosen to teach French in the Southern sectarian university on account of his moral integrity. High-principled colleges, he explained, could find few high-principled Frenchmen to teach their language and were forced to seek instructors among those of German stock.

Dr. Holt sent his family to his new post and, availing himself of his summer vacation, went himself to Central Park, near Hicksville, Long Island, where he rented a small, secluded cottage. He bought a hundred and twenty pounds of dynamite, a supply of fuses, blasting caps, fulminate of mercury, and various chemicals. He also bought two revolvers. In those casual days the right of the people to keep and bear arms and dynamite was not infringed upon. There is something of the sort in the Constitution.

Dr. Holt busied himself in his Long Island cottage with chemical research and target practice. He devised a simple and effective time bomb. In a packet of three sticks of dynamite he placed some fulminate-of-mercury caps. He inverted above the caps a corked vial of sulphuric acid. He carefully tested the time required for the sulphuric acid to eat its way through the cork and ignite the caps. By varying the thickness of the cork he could set the time of the explosion. (Some authorities insist that the bomb must have contained a fuse. If the authorities are right, it contained a fuse.)

Toward the end of June he left his Long Island retreat with a trunk and a suitcase. An expressman of Central Park recalled later the extraordinary weight of Dr. Holt's trunk and the doctor's insistence on sitting on it all the way to the station.

Dr. Holt sent his trunk to a storage warehouse at 342 West Thirty-eighth Street, in New York, and went on to Washington with his suitcase. On Friday, July 2, he visited the Capitol and stowed a bomb in a reception room adjoining the Vice President's office in the Senate wing. He took a berth on the

12:10 A.M. for New York. He retired when the waiting Pullman was opened, at 10 P.M., and, I like to think, lay listening in his berth. If this was what he was doing, he heard, shortly before midnight, a comforting boom from the Capitol.

In the morning papers, the story of the Capitol bomb overshadowed the news that the Russians had won a naval battle in the Baltic, that the Germans were storming the Argonne front, and that Charles Becker, New York police lieutenant under sentence of death for murder, was expected to tell something about some graft. The bomb did little damage. Plaster was shaken down, phone booths destroyed, mirrors and crystal chandeliers shattered. The morning papers also carried letters to the editor of a Washington paper from the dynamiter, supplying his own commentary on his act. His purpose, he announced, was only to call attention to the iniquity of shipping munitions to Europe. He had apparently written the letters the afternoon before in Washington. He chose the name "R. Pearce" for a signature.

Arriving in New York at 6 A.M., Dr. Holt breakfasted, read the morning papers, and took the 7:30 train for Glen Cove, Long Island. In Glen Cove he engaged a taxi to drive him to the estate of J. P. Morgan. "I am an old friend of Mr. Morgan's," he told the taxi driver. "If we happen to meet Mr. Morgan's car, signal to him to stop and just toss my suitcase into the back seat of his car."

The taxi drew up before the Morgan house. Holt, leaving his bag in the taxi, mounted the front steps and rang the bell. The butler, Henry Physick, answered the ring.

"I want to see Mr. Morgan," said Holt.

"What is your business with him?"

"I can't discuss that with you. I am an old friend of Mr. Morgan's. He will see me."

The hand of the mistrustful Physick was on the doorknob. But Holt reached in his coat pockets and flashed out a revolver in each hand.

"Where is Mr. Morgan?"

One is not J. P. Morgan's butler for nothing. "You will find Mr. Morgan in the library," said Physick calmly, pretending not to notice the revolvers. He turned to show the way —the wrong way. For Morgan was, in fact, in the breakfast room, at the opposite end of the house. There a pleasant meal was in progress. Mrs. Morgan was present, Sir Cecil Spring-Rice, the British ambassador, Lady Spring-Rice, and other guests.

"Upstairs, Mr. Morgan, upstairs!"

This extraordinary shout from the incomparable Physick chilled and muted the breakfast party and probably annoyed Dr. Holt. He apparently stood nonplused for a moment before starting in pursuit of his victim. Supposing that a burglar was on the second floor, most of the party hurried upstairs by a rear staircase to come to grips with him. They went from room to room, puzzled.

"A man is coming upstairs!" screamed Miss Rosalie McCabe, a nurse in the Morgan household, from the head of the main staircase.

The Morgans showed their mettle. They ran to the head of the stairs. Holt, still with a revolver in each hand, had reached the landing.

"Now, Mr. Morgan, I've got you!"

Mrs. Morgan sprang forward and threw herself before her husband. Morgan pushed her aside and, in a Morgan fury, ran down the stairs to deal with the fellow.

Holt fired twice, hitting Morgan, as has been mentioned, in the hip and groin. The financier, who weighed about two hundred and twenty pounds and who had the advantage of position, mass, and velocity, flung himself on Holt. The two came down on the landing, Morgan on top. He held one of the assailant's wrists; the other was pinned beneath the two men. Mrs. Morgan, Miss McCabe, and the British ambassador removed the wavering revolver from Holt's free hand. The admirable Physick delivered the *coup de grâce* with a heavy lump of fireplace coal on Holt's right temple. Morgan got up from the floor and someone slipped the second revolver out of Holt's hand.

Morgan telephoned his mother, who was in Utica, told her he was all right, and summoned a doctor and the police. Only then did he reveal that Holt's shots had wounded him.

In Holt's suitcase in the taxi were found two sticks of dynamite and two boxes of cartridges. A third stick of dynamite was picked up on the lawn. It had probably fallen from Holt's pocket.

Horrid with blood and coal, Holt was taken to the Mineola jail. Under rigorous questioning, he said that he had no intention of killing Morgan. He merely wanted to argue with him, to persuade him that the shipment of munitions to the Allies, a business in which Morgan was most extensively engaged, was evil. To aid in convincing the financier, he was prepared to seize as hostages Mrs. Morgan and the children, of whom the youngest was fourteen. His purpose was high; his shots had been fired merely in defense against unprovoked aggression.

"Don't you see that I didn't want to hurt him?" he said to reporters. "I wanted him to use his influence to prevent the exportation of arms and ammunition. I feel that you and I and everybody in this country who fails to use his influence to prevent the exporting of arms and ammunition is guilty of murder, since he contributes his part to the slaughter that is going on in Europe."

Holt insisted he was not pro-German. He was merely opposed to all war and to all murder. In his effects was found a letter to the Kaiser, protesting against the Emperor's "land-grabbing." Holt confessed voluntarily to placing the bomb in the Capitol and said it was designed only as publicity for pacifism.

Even the German-American press was shocked. America, almost whole-heartedly pro-Ally and pro-munitions-manufacture by that time, regarded Holt as crazy. He himself was half convinced of it.

"Do you think you are crazy?" said a detective to him.

"I don't know. Sometimes I do, sometimes I don't. I have been trying for six months to convince myself of one of two things—either that I am crazy or that I am not. I haven't been able to settle that question yet."

Just before Holt's day of crime he had posted a letter to his wife, revealing that he had been divinely commanded to check the munitions trade by striking the chief traders. Mrs. Holt subsequently turned over the letter to the authorities. They were startled, as were all newspaper readers who saw it, by one of his confidences. "A steamer leaving New York for Liverpool on July 3 should sink, God willing, on the 7th."

Meanwhile investigators had traced Holt's trunk and had found in it what New York's Inspector of Combustibles Owen Egan described as "the greatest equipment for bomb-making ever brought to New York." When the contents of the trunk were checked against Holt's purchases, fifty pounds of dynamite was found to be missing. All shipping was warned.

On the seventh, there was an explosion in one of the holds of the *Minnehaha*, a big liner bound from New York to Liverpool with a cargo of cordite and other munitions. She was brought safely into Halifax after two days of fighting the ensuing fire. Whether the explosion was caused by Holt's dynamite could never be settled.

Holt closed the case in his own way. He made an attempt at suicide by removing a lead-pencil eraser from its metal holder, biting the holder into a sharp edge, and with it trying to cut the artery in a wrist. The attempt was discovered and thwarted and a guard was stationed outside his cell in a gallery of the Mineola jail. The guard left the door unlocked in order to forestall any sudden attempt at suicide. On the night of the seventh, Holt was snoring convincingly. When some prisoners made a noise in another part of the cell block, the guard walked away to investigate. Holt immediately ran out of the cell, climbed up the criss-crossed bars of his cell door, and threw himself out over a gallery rail to a concrete floor eighteen feet below. His skull was fractured and he died immediately. After his death, identification by his brothers-in-law and others confirmed the suspicion that he was Erich Muenter.

J. P. Morgan next day was reported to be doing very nicely. He had sat up in bed, had been shaved, and had smoked a cigar.

Picture Credits